PRAYER JOURNAL *for* MEN

BIBLICAL LESSONS FROM LIVES OF 52 MEN

ANDERS BENNETT

TABLE OF CONTENTS

Introduction

Who is your hero? For many of us, there is a small list of men who we have looked up to. That list typically includes fathers and grandfathers. Oftentimes, pastors and Sunday School teachers are represented. Perhaps a good friend comes to mind. Whoever they may be, we all have people who we desire to emulate. Throughout this prayer journal, I hope to open your eyes to a few more men to add to your list.

The Bible is filled with men of great faith who are worth following. We're taught by Paul to learn lessons from the Old Testament. In 1 Corinthians 10:6, he says of Israel, "Now these things occurred as examples to keep us from setting our hearts on evil things as they did." Paul even goes on to say that we ought to emulate him as he follows Christ (1 Corinthians 11:1). Wonderfully, we find a whole list of men and women who are worthy of consideration in Hebrews 11. Scholars often call this chapter the "Hall of Faith." Since we have the example of Scripture and the command of Paul to look at the lives of the saints who have gone before us, it would be a valuable endeavor to spend a year studying the Men God uses.

While there are incredible women of the faith (like Hannah, Ruth, and Deborah) from whom we can and should learn, this study will focus on men for a couple of reasons. The first is that this prayer journal is designed for men. With men being the target audience, it makes sense for the examples to be godly men that will be examined.

The second reason is that the Bible places spiritual leadership in the hands of men. Paul holds Adam responsible for leading Eve in the Garden of Eden (1 Timothy 2:12-14). Every elder or pastor that is mentioned in the New Testament is a man, and the qualifications of the overseer are for a man (1 Timothy 3:1-7). The 12 disciples chosen by Jesus were all men, and the original deacons were men full of the Spirit (Acts 6:1-6). Husbands are called to love and lead their wives spiritually (Ephesians 5:25-27). Therefore, if spiritual leadership is what men are called to, it stands to reason that men would learn from men in Scripture.

Over 52 weeks, you will have the chance to examine the lives of 52 men in the Bible. You will see their successes and their failures. You'll learn from their life lessons that will be invaluable to your own. And ultimately, you'll see that they each will be pointing you to become more like Jesus. We are told that this is the grand plan of the Father; to conform us to the image of His Son (Romans 8:29-30). Jesus even reveals to His disciples that all of the Scriptures are written with Him in mind (Luke 24:27).

It is my prayer that you will use the guide through the Bible to help you grow in your knowledge of Scripture and your faith in the Savior. Allow each example not only to compel you to action but also to show you the fullness of Christ's life, death, and resurrection. May you be blessed by your time in the Word and your prayer with the Father.

How to Read Prayer Journal

To get the most out of this prayer journal, there are a few practical steps that are involved. However, more important than those steps is the attitude in which you approach your time in this book. The Bible says about itself that it is "*alive and active. Sharper than any double-edged sword, it penetrates even to divide soul and spirit, joints and marrow; it judges the thoughts and attitudes of the heart*" (U.S. Hebrews U.S.4:12). If this is true, then we can expect that every time we open God's Word, it will penetrate our hearts.

This will not happen, however, if we don't come to it humbly and are ready to receive what it has to say. You see, the Holy Spirit is what makes the Word of God so powerful. He is the One who is doing the work as you read His Word. But the Bible also says, "God opposes the proud but shows favor to the humble" (James 4:6). Therefore, when we come to read and study God's word, we must come with a humble posture. We must be ready to learn and grow in His timing and not our own. With this heart posture in mind, you can follow the three stages successfully.

Stage 1: Weekly Devotion

Each week, there will be a devotion that is based on the life of one of the men of Scripture. The Scripture that tells their story will be referenced, and a reflection on what their lives show us will be recorded below. You can take in this information in a handful of ways.

You can spend part of your week reading the Scripture first and the rest of the week reading and meditating on the devotion. You can begin your week with the devotion as a primer for your Bible reading.

Or you can re-read the devotional daily. I would encourage you to try a few different methods to see which one works the best for you.

Stage 2: Daily Prayer Journal Prompts

To get the most out of this book, you will need to utilize the journaling section. For a lot of men, journaling can be difficult. I want you to push yourself and embrace the process. Even if you only write down a few words or a few sentences, it will help you to process the Scripture and let it impact your life. Each day of the week, you'll have a prompt to respond to. Your journaling can be based on your thoughts on the Scripture, or it can be a time for you to write out your prayers.

Stage 3: Prayer Requests/Answers

This final stage of the process will end up being the most encouraging to you. Each week, you will have a place to write down various prayer requests. As you work your way through, make a note of how and when the Lord answered those requests. At the end of the year, you will have an awe-inspiring record of God's goodness in your life.

WEEK 1

ADAM - THE FIRST MAN

"Therefore, just as sin entered the world through one man, and death through sin, and in this way death came to all people, because all sinned."
ROMANS 5:12

Read Genesis 1-3

What makes a man a man? This question has flabbergasted our society. Depending on who you ask, you may get wildly different answers. Navigating those conversations as a Christian has become increasingly difficult. However, the confidence we can have is not in our intellect or influence. The confidence we can have is in the Bible. We can go to the source and read about the first man. In the story of Adam, we can see how God designed the first man and called him "good."

As you read Genesis 1-2, you'll see that Adam had two main functions in relationship with his wife, Eve. He was to provide for her and lead her. We see that he was to be a provider based on the job that God gave him. God told Adam to tend to the field and cultivate the garden. He was placed in the Garden of Eden to maintain and benefit from it. Even after the curse that comes in Genesis 3, Adam's function of being a provider remains. The job just becomes harder. It's with thorns and thistles that he will cultivate the ground.

The second job that Adam is given is to be a leader. Specifically, he was supposed to lead Eve spiritually. It was Adam who was given all of the commands from God. It was his job to relay that information accurately to Eve. It was his job to watch over Eve and make sure she followed the commands of God. This is why Paul holds Adam responsible for Eve eating the forbidden fruit in the Garden. Although he did not take the first bite, he took the first step away from leading her.

Today, those jobs still define a godly man. He will be someone who provides for others and leads others. How a man goes about doing that may look vastly different from Adam. Adam was a gardener by trade. This does not mean that all godly men are to be gardeners. But it does mean that we are to make sure our family is provided for. In some relationships, the best way for the family to be provided for is for the wife to be the main breadwinner. That is fine as well. But the man ought to be pulling his weight in some way or another.

Also, godly men today have the responsibility of leading others spiritually. This does not mean that all men are to be Sunday School Teachers, Deacons, or Pastors. There is a good reason that these jobs are limited to gifted men. But it does mean that in our circle of influence, we ought to be leading others to become more like Jesus. This may look like leading a Bible study or simply being a godly influence when you are on the golf course.

Godly men are providers and leaders. We don't all look the same. We don't have the same talents. We don't have the same callings. But we all have the same blueprint to follow. As we stick to God's word, we cannot go wrong when we follow His design for men.

REFLECTION

Day 1: What do you think it means to be a man?

To be a leader, a provider & Spiritually mature Christian

Day 2: How does Genesis 1-3 change or reinforce what you think about being a man?

Responsible to lead, guide & provide spiritual covering

Day 3: How has God equipped you to be a provider?

A job, a mindset to strive for success, a peaceful mind

Day 4: In what ways can you be a leader in your own home?

Inspire people to get knowing with God, be an example, Be like Christ

Day 5: What examples of godly men do you have to follow in your own life?

Pastor, parent, friends, biblical characters

Day 6: What bad examples of manhood have you witnessed?

friends parents leaving them [illegible] them

Day 7: Write a prayer to God about how you want to grow in your manhood?

PRAYER REQUESTS

ANSWERED PRAYERS

WEEK 2
CAIN - ANGER

""In your anger do not sin": Do not let the sun go down while you are still angry."
EPHESIANS 4:26

Read Genesis 4 from Cain's perspective.

Adam and Eve had three children that are named in Scripture. They had far more than this in totality, but the storyline of the Bible centers on these three. When Adam and Eve sinned, everyone who would be born after that would have a sinful nature in them. We are all sick with sin from the moment we exit our mother's wombs. By nature, we are selfish, and we see that clearly in the lives of Cain and Abel.

As you will read in Genesis 4, Cain murders his brother, Abel. He was upset that God accepted Abel's offering while rejecting his own. There is some speculation about why God would reject one and accept the other. The most consistent teaching in Scripture would lead us to the conclusion that Abel's offering was given in faith while Cain's was given with an impure motive.

God tells Cain that Abel's blood cries out for revenge from the ground after Cain cries out the famous question, "Am I my brother's keeper?" What a question for us to wrestle with this week. Are we our brother's keeper? To what extent are we watching out for the people in our lives? What should we be doing to do that? I think the answer begins in doing what Cain could not.

Cain could not manage his anger. It overwhelmed him, and he lashed out to kill his brother. Had Cain managed his anger, he would not have sinned in this way. We have the responsibility to "be angry and not sin" (Ephesians 4:26-27). This means that there is such a thing as righteous anger. But even righteous anger should not lead us towards sinful actions.

But the reality of the situation is that we rarely are angry over righteous things. Cain was angry because God was just. God accepted Abel's sacrifice given in faith. This is how God operates, and Cain knew that. But Cain wanted God to treat him differently. Cain wanted God to bless him despite the quality of his offering or his motivation. When that didn't happen, his anger festered.

It is at this moment, the moment of anger, that we need to step back and ask two questions. The first is, "Are we angry for righteous reasons or selfish reasons?" If they are selfish reasons, then we have the responsibility for placing that anger at the feet of Jesus and stepping away from the situation.

However, if we are angry for righteous reasons, we need to ask a second question: "How would Jesus respond to this situation?" More times than not, Jesus responded to situations that called for anger humbly. In Matthew 5:38-39, Jesus teaches the concept when someone strikes you on the cheek, you ought to turn the other cheek. This means that your first reaction in your anger should not be to lash out but to give the benefit of the doubt.

REFLECTION

Day 1: What does your anger look like? Do you lash out or keep it all inside?

Day 2: What tends to make you angry?

Day 3: How can you better control your anger?

Day 4: What situation in your life right now is causing you to become angry?

Day 5: When was the last time you were angry for righteous reasons?

Day 6: How would you answer the question, "Am I my brother's keeper?"

Day 7: Who in your life do you need to be looking out for?

PRAYER REQUESTS

ANSWERED PRAYERS

Week 3
Abel - Humility

"Do nothing out of selfish ambition or vain conceit. Rather, in humility value others above yourself."
Philippians 2:3

Read Genesis 4 from Abel's perspective.

This is your second week thinking about these verses of Scripture, but I am asking you to put yourself in Abel's shoes this time to see it from another perspective. As of right now, there are only two sons that are mentioned in the very first family on earth. There are no set norms or expectations to follow. And Abel has been chosen to be the shepherd of the family, while Cain is the gardener.

Abel was gifted in his job and gave glory and praise to God for it all. We see this as evidenced in what he offered to the Lord. The Bible says that he gave his firstborn to the flock. The first of all that he had; he gave to the Lord. He did not wait until the end of the season to see what was left over. He did not pick the runt of the litter. He gave God the first in expectation that God would provide the second and the third.

This faith, as mentioned last time, was a marked difference behind Abel's sacrifice in comparison to Cain. Perhaps one of the marks of Abel's life that we ought to consider this week was his humility. We do not read anything about Abel boasting about the Lord accepting his sacrifice over his brothers. The jealousy and anger that exists in the heart of Cain do not seem to be at the hands of Abel.

In this, we can be the kind of men that God uses. We can be men marked by humility. This kind of humility was seen not only in Abel's ife but also in the life of Jesus. Paul describes the humility of Jesus in Philippians 2:6-8 where he says, "Who, being in very nature God, did not consider equality with God something to be used to his advantage; rather, he made himself nothing by taking the very nature of a servant, being made in human likeness. And being found in appearance as a man, he humbled himself by becoming obedient to death, even death on a cross!"

If Jesus, the Lord of all Creation, can humble Himself to the point that He was willing to die for us, what could be our excuse for prideful actions? There simply is no reasonable excuse. We must have the mind that Christ had and put others before ourselves. We must have the mind that Christ had and not be boastful in our relationship with God.

As you work your way through this book and talk with others about what the Lord is doing in your life, you may be tempted to boast about your accomplishments. Beware of this, friend. For Abel did not boast in the Lord's acceptance of his sacrifice. He kept his head down and continued to be faithful to the task at hand. When you're tempted in this way, look to the cross and be reminded of the sacrifice of your Savior, which was accepted on your behalf.

REFLECTION

Day 1: How would you define humility?

Day 2: Who in your life is an example of humility?

Day 3: Why would Abel have been tempted to boast in his offering?

Day 4: What areas of your life are tempted to boast about?

Day 5: Why are we tempted to show false humility when given a compliment?

Day 6: What does it look like for someone to humbly accept praise?

Day 7: What do you admire the most about Jesus' humility?

PRAYER REQUESTS

ANSWERED PRAYERS

Week 4
Noah - Faithful

"Now it is required that those who have been given a trust must prove faithful."
1 Corinthians 4:2

Read Genesis 6-8

The world spiraled out of control ever since Adam and Eve sinned in the Garden of Eden. The first recorded event after that moment was a brutal murder that happened between their children. Things did not get any better. By the time you make it to Genesis 6, the world has devolved into utter sinfulness. So riddled with sin that God had decided to wipe everyone out and begin again. That was until He considered Noah.

Noah was a righteous man. He still had faith in God. We see this because Noah accepted a ridiculous task. Before a single drop of rain had ever fallen, Noah was told to build an enormous ark that would house 2 of every animal and a few extras of some special types. It was meant to be a zoo that floats and would need to be durable enough to last 40 days and 40 nights of rain with a subsequent 120 days of waiting on the water to recede. It was no small task.

Without a doubt, along the way, Noah was called all kinds of names. Each person who would walk by surely wagged their head and scoffed. Remember, the world was full of sinful people, and no one seemed to have faith apart from Noah. It is very likely that Noah's own family struggled to have faith in this situation.

And yet Noah was faithful, and so was God. At the right time, the rain began to pour, and Noah housed his family and the animals in the Ark. What a goal to set before us this week. When the Lord searched the earth for a sign of spiritual life, it was Noah who stuck out. It makes me wonder what the Lord would see if he looked in our town or in our home. Would we stick out among the crowd?

We are called to be men of faith. This means that we practice the definition given of faith in Hebrews 11:1, which says, "Now faith is confidence in what we hope for and assurance about what we do not see." Elsewhere, Peter describes faith like this: "Though you have not seen him, you love him; and even though you do not see him now, you believe in him and are filled with an inexpressible and glorious joy" (1 Peter 1:8). As men of faith, we must put all of our hope in one person. The One whom we have yet to see face to face, but one day we will stand before.

This kind of faith can be hard to hold onto. Its strength can come and go in waves. This is why it's not the strength of our faith that matters the most. It's the strength of the object of our faith. This is the wonderful thing about following Jesus. When we place our faith in Him, He places us in the palm of His hand and refuses to let go. Even in difficult seasons when our faith seems to be all but gone, there He will be, ever holding on.

REFLECTION

Day 1: What is your definition of faith?

Day 2: What would you have done if God told you to build an ark?

Day 3: How do you handle those who cast doubt on you?

Day 4: What can you do to fight doubt in your own heart?

Day 5: Describe a situation where you have had to have a strong faith.

Day 6: What happened in a situation when you failed to have faith?

Day 7: Take time to write a prayer asking God to strengthen your faith.

PRAYER REQUESTS

ANSWERED PRAYERS

Week 5

Abraham - Chosen

"But you are a chosen people, a royal priesthood, a holy nation, God's special possession, that you may declare the praises of him who called you out of darkness into his wonderful light."
1 Peter 2:9

Read Genesis 12 and 15

Abraham is known as the Father of Nations because of the incredible covenant that God made with him. It was originally recorded in Genesis 12 and is expanded on in Genesis 15. It boils down to three essential parts. He is promised a people, a place, and protection.

The people turn out to be the people of God, first seen in Israel and ultimately seen in the Church. The place is first fulfilled as they take the land of Canaan, called the Promised Land. This will be ultimately fulfilled as all the saints of God enter into the gates of Heaven. Finally, the protection is experienced in Abraham's lifetime and extends to God's people forever. He will always be on their side.

It would be worthwhile to spend time diving into the depths of these promises and see how exactly they are fulfilled, but what I want you to notice this time is what Abraham did to earn these promises. Go back and look. Maybe go back to chapter 14 and see what you can find. Did you see anything?

The incredible truth about how God interacts with us is that it is based on grace. God chose Abraham to be the recipient of this eternity-altering promise based solely on His grace. Abraham was not described as a particularly righteous man like Noah. He wasn't known as an avid church-goer or Bible reader. All we know of him is that

God chose him.

This incredible truth needs to penetrate our hearts as men. Men are typically task-driven, hands-on type people. We are, by nature, fixers. If something falls apart, we do our best to step in and fix the situation. However, when we fail to fix something, it can crush us. The expectation of being able to save the day can be overwhelming.

So much so that we are tempted never to step in. The fear of failure can be paralyzing to us in so many ways. But this is remedied when we see how God relates to us. It is not based on our performance. He is not impressed with our good work. He doesn't need us to fix anything. He has chosen to love us out of His abundant grace.

There is a wonderful freedom that awaits us when we walk in this freedom. It is not a license to live however we would like. It just removes the guilt and shame when we fail and pushes us towards faithful obedience. Imagine how your life would change if you related to others more on grace than work. What would be different if you chose to love people first before you expect any kind of performance out of them? How much better would life be if that is what people did with you? Dear brothers, our God has set His love on you. By His grace, you are chosen.

REFLECTION

Day 1: What other promises has God made to us in Scripture?

Day 2: What promise do you need to hear from God today?

Day 3: How does being chosen change how you view yourself?

Day 4: How does being chosen change how you view God?

Day 5: What would be different if you choose to love people first?

Day 6: In what ways does being chosen help you be a better spouse/friend?

Day 7: Write a prayer of praise for God's grace in choosing you.

PRAYER REQUESTS

ANSWERED PRAYERS

WEEK 6
LOT - PRIDE

"Pride goes before destruction,
a haughty spirit before a fall."
PROVERBS 16:18

Read Genesis 18-19

Abraham pleads with God on behalf of Lot, who lives in Sodom. The city, along with Lot and his family, is riddled with sin. Pride is overflowing everywhere. And yet Abraham steps in and cries out to God to spare the city. They make a deal that if there are 10 righteous men in the city, God will spare them.

But the judgment is cast. There is no one righteous in the city, "no, not one." Not even Lot. Every single one of them has earned the judgment of God. It's time for the angels to pull out, right? The mission is over. Abort and let the fire fall, right!? But the angel grabs Lot by the hand (make a note of that), pulls him inside to safety, and strikes the mob with a blinding light. They save Lot's life.

Then, they tell him to gather his family because the patience of God is coming to an end. They need to leave now. Lot runs to tell his sons and daughters, but they laugh on his face, thinking he is joking. The angels insist it's time to go NOW! Get your wife and two daughters, and let's go! You would think that would spur Lot into action, but his losses and get out of there, but the Scriptures say that he lingered.

That's it! He blew it! He had his second chance, and now he's left for dead. The angels are done with wicked Lot. It's got to be over now, right? Not so. Twice, the angels took these wretched people by the hand and saved their lives. God's patience and mercy have been overflowing.

The story of Lot in Sodom highlights two things: We are selfish people, and God is indescribably patient. In our selfishness, we tend to hurt other people. We put them in danger while taking care of ourselves. This is no way for a godly man to live. If you look at Jesus, it's the opposite approach that He took.

Instead of staying away from danger, Jesus went to the cross for us. He embraced and endured the danger that would end His life for the sake of others. In His humility, He displayed the indescribable patience of God. He has all authority to rain down fire from Heaven, and yet He waits. He patiently waits until He has drawn all of His people to Himself.

Let's not allow our lives to be marked by pride. Let's not let our actions and motivations endanger the ones we love. Rather, let's live dangerous lives that put others first. Let's be willing to take the blame, punishment, and bullet so that others can have peace.

REFLECTION

Day 1: Who in your life do you need to pray for?

Day 2: How can you step in and selflessly help them this week?

Day 3: Why is humility a dangerous way to live?

Day 4: What areas of your life do you struggle to be humble in?

Day 5: How does God's patience change your view of Him?

Day 6: Who do you need to be more patient with this week? How can you do that?

Day 7: In light of the Scripture, write a prayer to God telling Him what's on your heart.

PRAYER REQUESTS

ANSWERED PRAYERS

WEEK 7
ISAAC - DETERMINATION

"Let us not become weary in doing good, for at the proper time we will reap a harvest if we do not give up."
GALATIANS 6:9

Read Genesis 21-24

Isaac's birth was nothing short of a miracle. He was born to a couple that was well past child-bearing years. He was promised by God but unexpected by his parents. Sarah laughed at the thought of getting pregnant, and Isaac's name in Hebrew reflects that thought. Isaac grew up to be a lot like his dad, Abraham.

One of the things that they shared was their determination for those whom they loved. As you read the story of Isaac and Rebekah in Genesis 24, you'll see this on full display. He was willing to put in the literal work in order to have Rebekah as his wife. A lesser man would have given up after the first round of work. An even lesser man wouldn't have even tried to fight for the woman he loved. And yet Isaac put all of his effort into securing her for himself.

This is the kind of determination that needs to be present in every godly man. This doesn't have to show itself like it did in Isaac's life. We don't have to work year after year to gain a wife. But whatever we are called to do, we must do with all of our might. We must not give in just because things get difficult.

One of the reasons many men quit along the way is when an unexpected challenge arises. Instead of rising to the occasion and figuring out a solution, we are tempted to resign and use the unexpected situation as an excuse. Far be it from us, fellow man of God, to let an interruption in the plan God has for you to derail it all together.

When those challenges come, we must face them head-on. When they arrive, we need to pause for a moment. Pray about what the Lord would have us do. Ask for wisdom because we are promised it in the Word of God. Then, we must put together a godly plan. This may not be the plan of least resistance that we are drawn to. Sometimes, it is a plan that requires pain and conflict. But if we have the Lord's wisdom in our hearts and His prompting behind our actions, what could stop us? We're told in the Bible that if God is for us, then no one could stand against us.

Recently, I was training to run a 5k. My goal was to be able to run the race in under 30 minutes. I worked hard by waking up at 5:00 AM and working out with a few friends. Finally, when race day came, I hit a lot of unexpected challenges. The course had a lot of hills in it. It was hotter than I expected. And the person who was supposed to run with me bailed at the last minute. Needless to say, I had plenty of reasons to throw in the towel. By God's grace, I ran the race that morning and finished in first place in my age bracket.

I tell you this story not to puff myself up but to give an illustration of how God works. When we are working hard on what God has for us, He will see us through any difficulties that come our way.

REFLECTION

Day 1: Would you consider yourself a determined person? Why or why not?

Day 2: What areas of your life have had unexpected issues recently?

Day 3: When challenges arise, how do you typically respond?

Day 4: What can you do this week to show determination in your work life?

Day 5: How can you love your spouse or family with determination this week?

Day 6: Why does God reward the determination of His people?

Day 7: How can you encourage someone this week who is lacking determination?

PRAYER REQUESTS

ANSWERED PRAYERS

WEEK 8
ISHMAEL - REJECTED

"Now, Lord, consider their threats and enable your servants to speak your word with great boldness."
ACTS 4:29

Read Genesis 16 and 21

The story of Ishmael is tragic in a lot of ways. Due to someone else's sin, he was cast out as a reject for the majority of his young life. Because Abraham did not trust God, Ishmael was born of his mother, Hagar, the servant of Abraham. Because Sarah was jealous, Ishmael was treated unfairly in their home. Because Isaac was born, Ishmael and his mother were kicked out of the house altogether.

There came a point in Ishmael's life where he and his mom were going to die in the wilderness. They were lost, exhausted, and without water. Hagar and Isaac had laid down to die when an incredible thing happened. God spoke to Hagar and promised protection and blessing to her and Ishmael. The ones that were rejected by God's people were accepted by God Himself.

It's hard to imagine a more dramatic turn of events in the life of this young boy. His life was marked by rejection until God stooped down low, heard his cry, and accepted him. Have you ever felt like Ishmael? Have you gone through the pain of rejection? It's one of the scariest things that we face in life. From asking someone out on a date to applying for a job, rejection is painful when it comes.

Because rejection hurts, we are tempted to hide away. If we never put ourselves out there, we cannot be hurt through rejection. But if we believe the Gospel, then our view of rejection changes. The Bible teaches us that we are accepted by God, not rejected. When we place our faith in Jesus, we receive His grace. We are made righteous before God. Paul says it powerfully in Galatians 4:4-7 which reads, "But when the fullness of time had come, God sent forth his Son, born of woman, born under the law, to redeem those who were under the law, so that we might receive adoption as sons. And because you are sons, God has sent the Spirit of his Son into our hearts, crying, "Abba! Father!" So, you are no longer a slave, but a son, and if a son, then an heir through God."

We go from slaves to sons, the Bible proclaims. Therefore, if we are accepted by the Lord of all creation, the rejection we may face by man has very little consequence. Yet the pain will be there for the night, but joy comes in the morning. We can always look out and remember that we are accepted by God and feel His warm embrace in our souls.

And so, walk by faith in this life. Put yourself out there. Trust the Lord's acceptance of you will be enough. Live boldly and see what kind of doors God will open on your behalf. Be conscious of the pain of rejection when interacting with others, too. There are some people who are looking for a safe place to be themselves. Show them the love of God by being that safe place for them.

REFLECTION

Day 1: What time have you been rejected?

Day 2: What rejection are you fearful of today?

Day 3: How have you coped with rejection in the past?

Day 4: How does knowing you are accepted by God help you in your rejection by men?

Day 5: Is there someone in your life that you have rejected too harshly?

Day 6: How can you be a safe place for someone to open up to?

Day 7: What advice would you have given Hagar and Ishmael if you met them today?

PRAYER REQUESTS

ANSWERED PRAYERS

Week 9
Jacob - Bad Reputation

"A good name is more desirable than great riches; to be esteemed is better than silver or gold."
Proverbs 22:1

Read Genesis 27-33

Do you know anyone with a bad reputation? I remember my parents telling me to be careful who my friends were because one day, I would end up like them. There are some people that we ought to be on guard when we are around them. Jacob would have been one of those people.

Jacob was like a stereotypical politician. He would say whatever he needed to say to get what he wanted. He did exactly that in Genesis 27. He tricks his brother, Esau, into trading his birthright for a bowl of soup. Some of the blame certainly has to fall on Esau's shoulders. How absent-minded do you have to be to make that kind of mistake? But still, Jacob was the mastermind behind it all. He was the trickster, and Esau was the trickster.

As you read the story of Jacob, you'll see this same thing come back to bite him. He has a run-in with Laban like Isaac did. In that episode, Laban tricks Jacob. Later in Jacob's life, he is fearful of Esau and tries to butter him up (another way of tricking someone) by sending him gift after gift. Jacob even tries his hand at tricking God in a wrestling match that you can read about in Genesis 32.

Jacob had a bad reputation for taking advantage of people. He was a schemer. He was a weasel. He was also the next in line to receive the blessing of God. You see, Abraham was given a covenant. That covenant was passed from generation to generation. Isaac was privy to it, and Jacob was the next to receive it. You may think that God could have or should have removed the promise because of Jacob's poor behavior. But wonderfully, this is not how our God works.

Just like with Abraham, it was a covenant of grace. It was not based on how good or bad they were. It was based on how good God was. And because God is perfectly good, he would not break the promises He made to His people. God used Jacob in incredible ways. As you will read next week, God changed Jacob's name, and he became the literal father of the nation of Israel. What was promised to Abraham begins to take shape in the Trickster, Jacob.

The devil would love for you to believe that your past bad reputation is what defines you. He would love for you to count yourself out of the fight for God's kingdom. He whispers old lies in our ears like, "Did God really forgive you? Could God really use you? Surely not! He's got better people to work with. You need to sit down and keep your mouth shut."

That's not true, brother! There is only one perfect person that God used, and that person is His son Jesus. Everyone else in the Bible was sinful and fallen, too. And yet God took the sinful and fallen man and used him to bring Himself glory. This is exactly what God wants to do in your life as well. Your past, no matter how rotten, your reputation, no matter how sinful, will not keep God from using you for His glory.

REFLECTION

Day 1: Were you a good influence on others as a kid?

Day 2: Do you have anyone who looks up to you now?

Day 3: How can you use your influence to help others?

Day 4: What do you have to do to cover up for a bad reputation you have?

Day 5: How should that change how we treat people with bad reputations?

Day 6: What do you hope your reputation is now?

Day 7: What do you need to do to make sure that happens?

PRAYER REQUESTS

ANSWERED PRAYERS

Week 10
Esau - Tricked

"Bear with each other and forgive one another if any of you has a grievance against someone. Forgive as the Lord forgave you."
Colossians 3:13

Read Genesis 25 and 36

Esau was not faultless in how he was tricked, but he was still that: tricked. He was treated poorly by his brothers and robbed of a great blessing from his father. Maybe you've experienced something like this in your own life. Have you ever been on the wrong end of a deal?

One time, I was serving as the worship pastor at a local church. I made a friend there. We went to the same Bible study together. We shared meals together. We were buddies. At one point, he mentioned to me that he needed a new car. He had broken down beyond repair. As providence would have it, I was trying to sell a car. I was hoping to buy a truck and needed to sell my car first.

Seeing God's hand at work in bringing us together, I told him that I was selling my car, and I made him a great deal. The car was worth a couple thousand, but I sold it to him for one grand. We had a handshake agreement. The next week, we were signing papers and getting tags and titles figured out. However, I have not received any money yet. He told me he couldn't pay it all upfront. He said that he would pay it back in payments. Because we were friends and saw each other each week at church, I didn't think anything of it. Even if it took a while to get fully paid back, at least that money was coming eventually, right?

I was tricked. From that day on, I never saw him again. He was like a ghost. He was there one minute and gone the next. Because of that experience, I have my guard up during any financial transaction. I'm always worried that I'm being tricked because I have been tricked in the past.

We can get jaded when we get hurt. We can unfairly judge and react to people because of how we have been treated in the past. But the Gospel calls us to another way of life. The good news of Jesus is that we have been forgiven an impossible debt. God doesn't hold what we have done to Him in the past against us. The mercies received from Him are new every morning.

This means that we ought to show that same mercy to others in our lives. We have to retrain our minds, with the help of the Holy Spirit, to assume the best of others in our lives. Yes, we are more prone to being taken advantage of. Yes, it sets us up to be tricked or hurt again. But this is the life of Christ. He was tricked and taken advantage of. If He had not endured all that He had, we would have no hope of salvation.

Be wise, brothers. Don't fall because you're absent-minded like Esau. But be gracious and forgiving of those in your life. Seek to give above and beyond and see how God will bless you even when you're taken advantage of.

REFLECTION

Day 1: Can you think of a time when you were tricked?

Day 2: How quick or slow are you to forgive when you've been hurt?

Day 3: Are there certain people in your life that you refuse to forgive? Why?

Day 4: What truth in God's Word can you remind yourself of when you get hurt?

Day 5: How does this change your heart when you hurt others?

Day 6: Is there someone you need to seek out and apologize to this week?

Day 7: What would you say to the person who hurt you last if you could?

PRAYER REQUESTS

ANSWERED PRAYERS

WEEK 11

ISRAEL - NEW NAME

"Whoever has ears, let them hear what the Spirit says to the churches. To the one who is victorious, I will give some of the hidden manna. I will also give that person a white stone with a new name written on it, known only to the one who receives it."
REVELATION 2:17

Read Genesis 35

Do you have a nickname? In high school, I was given the nickname Frodo. That wasn't because I had a precious golden ring. It was because I was shorter than everyone in my class. As a wrestler, my size played to my advantage in many ways. But generally, my height was not my friend. My nickname reminded me of something I needed to overcome.

Jacob had the opposite experience of me. Jacob's given name meant "trickster." But the Lord changed his name. No longer would he be referred to by his birth name; he was to be called Israel. This name change was an important moment in Jacob's life and the life of God's people.

For God's people, it was the beginning of a new nation. Jacob's, now Israel's, sons would become the 12 leaders of the 12 tribes of the nation of Israel. The promise that was made so long ago to their forefather, Abraham, was beginning to take shape. When God said Abraham would be the father of nations, He had the nation of Israel in mind as His special people. It would be through Israel that His Son, Jesus, would come into the world.

But if we zoom back into Jacob's life, we can see the significance of this moment for him, too. This was a turning point for him. He was no longer going to live his old life. He was going to live the new life that God had for him.

There is a story about Jesus and a woman caught in adultery in John 8. The story goes like this: There was a woman who was dragged into the streets, having been caught in adultery. The religious leaders stood ready to stone her to death for the offense. They asked Jesus what He had to say on the matter. They were trying to get Him to say the wrong thing. Jesus famously wrote in the sand as He thought. Then He stood up and said, "He who is without sin can cast the first stone." One by one, the people dropped their stones.

This was the renaming moment for the woman who was caught in sin. She was forgiven a death sentence and then told by Jesus, "Go and sin no more." In other words, Jesus told her to leave her old life, her old name, behind and live up to the new name she had been given: forgiven.

Each one of us who has placed our faith in Jesus has been given a new name, too. We may still go by our birth name. That is right and good. But we are also called sons of God. We are called friends of the Father. We, too, are called forgiven. Let's live up to our new name. We should not take advantage of this gracious gift. We should be telling the world about the good news that we have found in Jesus. Let's tell them our new name.

REFLECTION

Day 1: Why did you get your nickname?

Day 2: Of all the names in Scripture given to believers, what is the most meaningful one to you?

Day 3: Why do you think God changed Jacob's name?

Day 4: Why didn't having a new name solve Jacob's problems?

Day 5: How did his new name change his life?

Day 6: If you could give yourself a new name, what would it be and why?

Day 7: Who can you tell this week about your new name in Christ?

PRAYER REQUESTS

ANSWERED PRAYERS

Week 12
Reuben - Compassionate

"Therefore, as God's chosen people, holy and dearly loved, clothe yourselves with compassion, kindness, humility, gentleness and patience."
Colossians 3:12

Read Genesis 37

This week, as you spend time on the story of Joseph, I want you to consider it from Reuben's vantage point. Joseph was one of twelve brothers, and he was clearly the father's favorite. There was no hiding that. He was the only son of the wife that he loved the most. Israel even gave Joseph a special coat to display his particular love for him.

This left the rest of the children filled with jealousy and resentment every time Joseph came around. Imagine how much these feelings would have been intensified when Joseph shared with his brothers the dreams that he had. He dreamed that all of his brothers and his parents would one day bow down to him. In the ears of his brothers, there could not be a more boastful and prideful statement to make.

In their anger, they concocted a plan to get rid of Daddy's favorite. Their first plan was nothing short of murder. They were simply going to kill him and dispose of the evidence. This is where Reuben steps in. His part in all of this is far from righteous. He hates Joseph just as much as his brother. However, within Reuben is a compassion that doesn't exist in his brothers.

You see, Reuben still loved Joseph even when he was frustrating to live with. He loved him simply because they were brothers. Reuben also loved his father. He didn't want his father to bear the loss of a son. Finally, Reuben loved God. He knew that murder was a heinous crime and did not want to stand before God with that on his record. This love for God and love for others compelled him to offer an alternative to his brothers.

Instead of killing Joseph, Reuben suggested they throw him in a pit and leave him to die. Reuben was hoping this would buy him enough time to smooth things over. But his plan ultimately backfired when a group of slave traders came by. In the end, they all agreed to sell Joseph into slavery.

Can you imagine being Reuben in his situation? There was a whirlwind of emotions to sort your way through. The dynamics of trying to lead his brother and save Joseph were delicate. It can be hard to know what to say and when to say it in emotionally charged situations. However, what guided Reuben's actions? It seems to be that compassion and love guided his steps. His love for God and others moved him to action.

Friend, there will be plenty of times in your life when you'll be unsure of what to do or what to say. In those moments, the best path forward is the one led by compassion. Choose the plan that loves God and others the most. Whatever that may be and however difficult it may seem. This will be the plan that God honors.

REFLECTION

Day 1: Why were the brothers justified in their anger?

Day 2: Why were their actions not justified?

Day 3: What would you have done if you were one of the brothers?

Day 4: What should Reuben have done?

Day 5: Do you have a situation in your life that is difficult?

Day 6: What can you do in that situation to love God the most?

Day 7: What can you do in that situation to love others the most?

Moses knew that when he approached Pharoah, he was putting his own life on the line. The Pharaohs of Egypt considered themselves to be gods. To submit to the will of another God would not be tolerated. It would be considered in the same line as treason. Moses' proposal to the Pharaoh could be taken poorly, and he could be killed on the spot.

Moses was scared. We all would have been, too. So, Moses made a few excuses to try to get out of it. The primary excuse that Moses used was that he was not a good public speaker. He said he couldn't lead anyone because he didn't speak well. If this was true, and that is a big "if" because Moses would have had the best education in the nation, it was not entirely revelation.

Moses did not have to be eloquent. He just needed to be obedient. His fears were based on what he could not do. They did not consider what God could do. When we're faced with fearful situations, we do the same thing. We spend all of our time thinking about what we cannot do. We worry about what others can do to us. And we fail to recognize what God can do.

Read the rest of Exodus, and you will see what God can do. God can split the Red Sea. He can send manna from Heaven. He can heal from venomous snake bites. He can defend from foreign armies. God can do anything He wishes. We have nothing to fear if He is for us.

REFLECTION

Day 1: Why did God choose Moses to lead the Exodus?

Day 2: Why did Moses feel scared about that?

Day 3: What other excuses could he have used?

Day 4: How did God answer those excuses?

Day 5: What conversations have you had that made you fearful?

Day 6: What would you say to yourself now that you know how it went?

Day 7: What verses of Scripture could you remind someone of when they are scared?

PRAYER REQUESTS

ANSWERED PRAYERS

Week 14
Aaron - Pressured

"Am I now trying to win the approval of human beings,
or of God? Or am I trying to please people?
If I were still trying to please people,
I would not be a servant of Christ."
Galatians 1:10

Read Genesis 32

Do you remember the excuse Moses gave before leading the Exodus of God's people from Egypt? It was that he was not a very good speaker. Do you remember how God answered that excuse? It was to give him a helper who would be a good speaker. That helper's name was Aaron. Aaron would go on to play an important role in the life of God's people.

There was a huge moment for Moses as he was leading them through the wilderness. God called Moses onto the mountain so that he could receive the Law from God. Moses spent a long time on the mountain writing down all that God had to say to him. The famous stone tablets that portray the 10 Commandments were a part of this whole process.

However, while Moses was on the mountain, someone had to be with the people. He was going to be away for over a month. Someone had to be the leader in his stead. In particular, someone had to be the spiritual leader of Israel. This was supposed to be Aaron's job. A job that he failed miserably. Let's consider how.

Put yourself in Aaron's shoes for a moment. God did not speak directly to Aaron as He did to Moses. God had not given him a plan and wasn't leading him. God was doing all of this with Moses. So, imagine the pressure that Aaron felt when Moses was gone for weeks, and the people began asking questions.

When he couldn't come up with answers, I'm sure they began demanding that he do something. So, what could he do? What was his point of reference? Well, they all knew what it meant to worship from their time in Egypt. The issue is that the worship they were familiar with was idol worship, which is explicitly forbidden by God.

Aaron, feeling the pressure from God's people, made a golden calf for them to worship. He crumbled under the weight of pressure from the crowd. Instead of holding onto what he knew, he guessed his way to a blunder.

Friend, there will be times in your life when you will be pressured by those around you. You may fear for your reputation. You may now know what to do. You may feel like the only way forward is to give in to whatever they want you to do. Take a lesson from Aaron's life. Don't give in. Maybe all you need to do is nothing. Look back to the last thing you knew to be right and wait for further instructions. You'll keep yourself out of trouble and those who follow you as well.

REFLECTION

Day 1: Why do you think Aaron made a golden calf?

Day 2: Why did Moses force them to drink the ashes of the calf?

Day 3: Why did God's people want something to worship?

Day 4: How would Moses have felt when he came off the mountain to find the calf?

Day 5: Would you have been able to withstand the pressure?

Day 6: How have you experienced pressure like this?

Day 7: When the pressure comes, what can you do to prioritize God?

PRAYER REQUESTS

ANSWERED PRAYERS

WEEK 15

NADAB AND ABIHU - WORSHIP

"God is spirit, and his worshipers must worship in the Spirit and in truth."
JOHN 4:24

Read Leviticus 10

Worship is incredibly important to God. Theologians have often said that the chief end of man is to worship God and enjoy Him forever. This is the very reason we were created. Since God desires for all men to worship Him, it stands to reason that He has a design for how He wants to be worshiped. This is a large reason why the book of Leviticus exists.

The Levites were charged with leading God's people in the worship of Him. All of the rules and regulations regarding sacrifices are laid out in this book. In the midst of it all, God tells us a story of the sons of Aaron and how they worshiped him. The two sons in focus are Nadab and Abihu.

As you read the story, you'll see that they offered incense unto the Lord in their worship of Him. That sounds innocent enough, but the incense they offered was "unauthorized." Some Bibles translate that they offered "strange fire" before the Lord. What exactly was unauthorized, we don't know. It could have been what they burnt or when they burnt it. But the point of the story is to say that it wasn't according to God's plan for worship.

The repercussions of this action can be shocking and confusing. They were consumed by fire from the Lord. There are two things that are significant about this. The first is that it was Through fire that they sinned and through fire that they were punished. God makes it clear that the reason for their death that day was that they did not worship how they were supposed to.

The second noteworthy thing is the seriousness of the worship of God. He does not take it lightly. If we fail to worship Him rightly, we accrue the penalty of death. It is a capital offense to commit treason against the King. He will not stand for it.

So, what does this mean for us today? Offering incense is no longer a common practice for Christians. What are we doing in response to this story? The big takeaway needs to be this. We have a holy responsibility to worship God how He wants. This means we need to study the Scriptures and see how His people are told to worship Him. This also means that we are to worship Him in purity of heart.

The next time you gather with your brothers and sisters at church, worship God with all that you have. Sing loudly. Pray humbly. Listen obediently. Worship God and lead others to do the same with you.

REFLECTION

Day 1: How do you worship God?

Day 2: Are there new ways to worship God you want to try?

Day 3: Why does God take worship so seriously?

Day 4: How can wrong worship be guilty of the death penalty?

Day 5: How do you worship when you go to church?

Day 6: How can you lead others to worship more passionately this week?

Day 7: What is your favorite worship song?

PRAYER REQUESTS

ANSWERED PRAYERS

Week 16
Joshua - Leader

"Be shepherds of God's flock that is under your care, watching over them - not because you must, but because you are willing, as God wants you to be; not pursuing dishonest gain, but eager to serve; not lording it over those entrusted to you, but being examples to the flock."
1 Peter 5:2-3

Read Joshua 1-5

God had been faithful. He promised that He would deliver His people to the Promised Land. It would be a land flowing with milk and honey. It would be for their possession so long as they obeyed and loved Him. So far, God has been leading His people through the person Moses. But as you have read, Moses passed away. The torch of leadership had been passed to Joshua. Joshua was not a random person. He had essentially been Moses' apprentice towards the end of his life. Joshua was being prepared for this moment of leadership.

But I can imagine that no amount of preparation can really be sufficient for such a task. Moses had led God's people out of Egypt, across the Red Sea, and through the wilderness. The second Joshua began to fail, the first phrase out of the mouths of the people would surely be, "Moses never did that!"

At the beginning of Joshua's leadership, God makes it clear to him how he will be successful. It will only be if Joshua listens to the Lord. Just as Moses had to fully submit to the word of God, so did Joshua. And that is exactly what Joshua did. Look at the whole book, and you'll see unwavering faith and commitment to the Lord in Joshua's life.

Maybe you've been put in a situation like this. I know I have. My very first position as a youth pastor was following my mentor, Peter. He did a wonderful job leading the youth ministry at the church. I was overwhelmed at the thought of trying to follow in his footsteps. For my very first lesson with the youth group, I actually taught Joshua 1. It was more like a lesson for me than for them. I knew what the Bible taught. If I was going to lead successfully, then my standard of success must not be a typical measure. It could not be how many students came to my group. It couldn't be how much money we raised for charities. It couldn't be a product. It had to be an attitude. The measure of success, according to the Bible, is obedience and faithfulness.

You may not be in a position of leadership right now. But you are surely being with someone. What standard do you hold them to? What are you looking for in order to call them a good or bad leader? Let me encourage you to begin using Joshua 1 as your basis. Instead of looking at the numbers first, look at the heart. Are they trying to be faithful and obedient? Are they using scripture to support why they are doing what they are doing? If they are, then they are successful leaders in the eyes of God.

If you are a leader, look at how and why you lead. Even if you don't lead in a ministry context, the bill's principles of leadership still remain. You can be a godly leader as a businessman or coach. Wherever the Lord has placed you, be faithful. Be obedient to His Word.

REFLECTION

Day 1: How are you leading in your own life?

Day 2: In what ways do you feel the weight of leadership?

Day 3: Who is leading you?

Day 4: How would you describe their leadership?

Day 5: In order to be more biblical, how should they change?

Day 6: What are things you need to change about your life to be more biblical?

Day 7: What did Jesus' leadership look like?

PRAYER REQUESTS

ANSWERED PRAYERS

WEEK 17
BALAK - LISTEN TO GOD

"My son, pay attention to what I say;
turn your ear to my words. Do not let them out
of your sight, keep them within your heart."
PROVERBS 4:20-21

Read Numbers 22-24

Have you ever had an experience where you felt strongly that the Lord had spoken to you in a supernatural way? I can remember when I was in high school and at the youth summer camp, the Lord spoke to me. It was that summer that he called me into ministry. He made it clear to me that he wanted me to serve him in the local church. At that time, I didn't really know how that would work and what that would look like, but I was confident that that is what he had said to me on the beach that night.

Most of the time, God does not speak to us like this. He has given us his word for a reason. It is a sure and concrete thing. We can know what God thinks and believes as we read his word in black and white. But there are moments even in Scripture that are supernatural. God chooses to speak through circumstances and situations. That is the case with the story of Balak.

This story gives me a lot of confidence. God chose to speak through a donkey to his servant. That gives me confidence because there are many times when I feel like I have fallen short in sharing the word of God with others. But if he can speak through a donkey, then he can surely speak through me.

What is noteworthy about this story is that God would not stop until Balak finally listened. In order to get his attention, he shook him up and opened his eyes to the reality around him. Sometimes, this is what God has to do for us in order for us to listen to him. Let's Be honest. We are not the most attentive people.

There are many things in this world that can be distracting to us. We have our personal lives and our social lives to think about. We have our professional lives that are taking our time. And at the end of the day, it seems as if we simply have lost all the time to think about our savior. Or we have not taken the time and preserved the time to hear from him.

As men of God, we ought to guard our hearts against the distractions of this world. Yes, there are plenty of things that are vying for attention. And yes, these things deserve our attention from time to time. But there should be nothing more important to us than speaking to and hearing from the creator of the universe. He loves us so much that he gave us his word in a book. We can hear from him whenever we want. Be sure to take time to listen to him today.

REFLECTION

Day 1: What is significant about God speaking through a donkey?

Day 2: How does God speak to us today?

Day 3: What is the last thing you remember learning from Him?

Day 4: What was that experience like?

Day 5: How can you help others hear from the Lord?

Day 6: What distractions exist in your own life?

Day 7: How can you remove or ignore those distractions this week?

PRAYER REQUESTS

ANSWERED PRAYERS

WEEK 18
OTHNIEL - DELIVERER

"The Spirit of the Lord is on me, because he has anointed me to proclaim good news to the poor. He has sent me to proclaim freedom for the prisoners and recovery of sight for the blind, to set the oppressed free."
LUKE 4:18

Read Judges 1-2

God's people were in trouble a lot. They seemed to find themselves in difficult situations. They were often at war with foreign nations. However, they were not unlucky. They were in trouble because they had sinned against God. The foreign nations were oftentimes a form of discipline from God.

I can remember a time when my brother and I were pulled over by a police officer on the way to the store. We were going to get a new toy. When the officer pulled us over, it was not his fault that we were stopped. It was our fault for having sped. The same is true of the Israelites. It was their fault that they were having such issues with war.

But God never leaves his people alone. He always provides a way of salvation. In the Book of Judges, it is through these judges that God delivers His people. The first one that is mentioned in the book is Othniel. Othniel was your typical judge in this book. He was a warrior/savior. He quite literally saved the lives of the Israelites.

As you read your way through this book, you will notice a pattern. You will see the sin of Israel. You will see the punishment brought by the hands of a foreign nation. You'll see God's people cry out for help. And you will see God answer their prayer with a judge. That judge will deliver God's people, and they will praise him for a short time.

But then they will go back to their sinful lives. Sadly, as you make your way through this book, you will see that cycle get faster and faster. The repentance and praise are short-lived. And God's people become more and more wicked and sinful.

Reading the Book of Judges can give you a jaded view of God's people. It can make you wonder and question how they could end up that way. But that is not the point of the book. The point of the book is to show us our need for an even greater judge. It is to show us our need for an even greater deliverer. And that delivery came in the person of Jesus Christ.

This means that the person in the Book of Judges that you ought to relate to the most is not the deliverer. It is not the judge. The person that you should relate to the most is the sinful Israel. In the grand scheme of our story, that is who we are. We are the sinful ones who need to be saved from our sins. And just as God was faithful to always send a deliverer to his people, he is faithful to send a deliverer to you today.

REFLECTION

Day 1: How have you noticed the cycle of Judges playing out in your life?

Day 2: Why does God always deliver His people?

Day 3: Why does God deliver His people through a person and not a power?

Day 4: What lessons did you learn from Othniel in your study?

Day 5: Spend time writing a prayer of thanksgiving for deliverance today.

Day 6: Who can you share your story of deliverance with?

Day 7: How did sharing your story go?

PRAYER REQUESTS

ANSWERED PRAYERS

Week 19
Ehud - Warrior

"Put on the full armor of God, so that you can take your stand against the devil's schemes."
Ephesians 6:11

Read Judges 3

There are moments in the Bible that are simply comical. For example, there is a story of a man who is made fun of for being bald. That man, in his anger, pleads for God to intercede. And the offenders were eaten by bears. There is a whole lot to unpack with that story, and we do not have time to do that in this Bible study. But the point is this: God works in unusual ways, and sometimes those ways are simply funny.

That is the case with the story of Ehud. Ehud was a left-handed man who was sent by God to kill the foreign king. However, this foreign king was so large that when Ehud went to go and stab him, his fat swallowed the sword hole. The death of somebody is never a funny thing. But the way in which this foreign king died has got to make you chuckle at least a little bit.

Although it was a funny thing, what Ehud had to do was indeed a very brave thing. It took a considerable amount of courage. At the end of the day, Ehud was sent to assassinate the most powerful man in the area. Had he made even one mistake, he would have lost his own life. Ehud was a warrior. He was a warrior who fought for the Lord.

God is not calling men to assassinate kings any longer. However, he still calls men to be warriors for his name. The Bible describes that we are to put on the full armor of God each and every day. It tells us plainly that we are in the midst of spiritual warfare. And that spiritual warfare typically happens in the midst of flesh and bone. There are men and women who would see the name of God be dragged through the mud. As his warriors, we are to defend his holy and great name.

We do not defend his name through physical violence. We defend His name by simply standing on the word of God. When His name and His word are called into question, we boldly and lovingly speak the truth. This requires, however, that we know the truth. This means that we must be familiar with God's word.

Suppose someone were to stop you on the street. If that person were to ask you why you believe in the Bible, would you have an answer for them? What would you say if they asked you for the reason for your hope in Jesus? These are important questions that you need to be prepared to answer. This does not mean that you need to become a theologian or Bible scholar overnight. But it does mean that you need to take your faith seriously. Do not be fooled, brothers. The Christian life is a life of war.

REFLECTION

Day 1: How can you become prepared to defend your faith?

Day 2: What areas of your faith are you still unsure of?

Day 3: Take time today to read about Christian Apologetics.

Day 4: What did you learn about Christian Apologetics yesterday?

Day 5: When might you need to defend your faith this week?

Day 6: How can you stand up for God while still loving your neighbor?

Day 7: Where can you look for the courage to do this?

PRAYER REQUESTS

ANSWERED PRAYERS

WEEK 20

BARAK - HANDS OF ANOTHER

"Two are better than one, because they have a good return for their labor. "
ECCLESIASTES 4:9

Read Judges 4-5

The one and only female judge was named Deborah. It is not clear in the scripture why she is the one and only. We know that she was righteous and fair and was able to judge the issues of her day. But in comparison to every other judge, she is very different. She was not a warrior like the others. And she was not a man like the others.

Since this is a book written primarily for men, we will not spend much time considering Deborah. But we will consider the man who worked alongside her. His name was Barak. His role in the story is a subservient role. He was Deborah's helper. The idea that she had, he accomplished.

We know people like this in our own lives. They are not the leader, but they often carry out the actions of the leader. They're the hands of another. Without them, the plan cannot succeed. Therefore, the relationship between Deborah and Barack is really interesting. Deborah is clearly marked as the judge and deliverer. But Barack is the one who does much of the work.

If you find yourself in a subservient role, do not be dismayed. It does not mean that you are unimportant. And it does not mean that God cannot use you. In fact, God may be using you to do the physical action of the idea that he placed in another. You do not have to be the leader to be important. Both Deborah and Barack were necessary for the deliverance of God's people.

If you find yourself in a leadership role, do not take advantage of those who do the grunt work. They are just as necessary to accomplishing the task as you are. While you may get more accolades for coming up with ideas and orchestrating plans, they are the ones who do a lot of legwork. At the end of the day, God works through teams of people. Each of those members has a job to do, and they are all important.

God describes his church as the body of Christ. He also says that it would be foolish for the entire body to be made up of eyes or ears. If it didn't have the various parts, then it would severely lack what it needed. The same is true in our lives. We need leaders and followers. We need thinkers and doers. We need men and women.

The next time you are serving with a team, take time to appreciate those who are around you. Make a note of their strengths and their weaknesses and see if you can pair people together that will serve one another. Be strategic in who you work with and who you work for. With the right team around you and a God-given plan, you can accomplish anything that he sets out for you to do.

REFLECTION

Day 1: Would you call yourself a leader or a helper?

Day 2: In what areas of your life are you a helper?

Day 3: How can you help others more than you currently do?

Day 4: How can you thank those who serve you this week?

Day 5: Why does God choose this couple to deliver His people?

Day 6: What about this story did you not expect?

Day 7: What lessons did you learn from this passage of Scripture?

PRAYER REQUESTS

ANSWERED PRAYERS

Week 21
Gideon - Weak

"But he said to me, "My grace is sufficient for you, for my power is made perfect in weakness." Therefore I will boast all the more gladly about my weaknesses, so that Christ's power may rest on me."
2 Corinthians 12:9

Read Judges 6-8

One of the main reasons that I love sports is because of the stories of men and women who come out of nowhere and become star players. If you have followed sports for any length of time, you have seen this kind of thing play out. It is incredible to see someone with no reputation all of a sudden rise to fame because of the spectacular performance.

In the story of Gideon, this is the kind of thing that we see play out. Gideon is a self-admitted, weak man. He does not come from a strong and powerful family. This is one of the excuses he uses when God calls him to be the next judge and deliverer for his people. He knows where he comes from, and he knows that no one is impressed with him. However, God shows favor to Gideon.

What is really interesting about the story of Gideon is that God does not give him Incredible strength to overcome his enemies. God himself is his strength. God is the one that does the fighting on his behalf. It is interesting that God does not eliminate Gideon's weakness. Rather, God becomes the very thing that Gideon needs the most.

Where is a powerful lesson in Gideon's life for us today? What we would like for God to do is eliminate our weaknesses. The hardships and shortcomings that we face in life, and we would rather God simply take care of them. But that is not often how God works. God loves to display His Glory by showing his own strength despite our weaknesses.

Maybe this story of how God uses Gideon to save his people will inspire you with a new kind of prayer. Instead of praying for God to remove the issues in your life, maybe you need to begin praying that God would simply use you. However, he sees fit and whenever he sees fit to do so. What God wanted more than anything out of Gideon was not his strength. It was not his intellect nor his physical ability. What God wanted and what God still wants today is our hearts. He wants us to be willing to be used by him. He simply wants us to trust him.

What is it that God is calling you to do today? What are the excuses that you have been giving him? What are the weaknesses that you have been hiding behind? Trust the god of Gideon. Trust the god that you claim to follow. Whatever he calls you to do and wherever he commands you to go, go with full confidence. For God will not lead you without providing for you what you need.

REFLECTION

Day 1: What are some of the excuses you give to not serve God?

Day 2: How could God overcome your weakness to show his strength?

Day 3: Is there someone in your life who needs this kind of encouragement?

Day 4: Why do you think God wants to use weak people to do strong things?

Day 5: Over your lifetime, how has God proven to be strong for you?

Day 6: How does Gideon's story change how you pray about the difficulties in life?

Day 7: Who else in the Bible does God work this way with?

PRAYER REQUESTS

ANSWERED PRAYERS

WEEK 22
SAMSON - SACRIFICE

"Therefore, I urge you, brothers and sisters, in view of God's mercy, to offer your bodies as a living sacrifice, holy and pleasing to God–this is your true and proper worship."
ROMANS 12:1

Read Judges 13-16

There are many lessons that you could learn from the life of Samson. You could learn lessons about what it is to fight temptation. You could learn about the destruction of sin. You could learn about the dangers of following your heart as opposed to following what God would have you do. But the lesson that I want us to see in the life of Samson is one that comes at the end of his life.

In order to understand the impact of his sacrifice, we have to think about the overall story of Samson. In short, God gives Samson physical strength so long as he does not break the vow that he made to him. Now, many times in Samson's life, he breaks that vow. But the straw that broke the camel's back so to speak, is when Samson allows his hair to be cut. At the moment that his hair is cut, he loses his strength, and he is captured.

But there is this wonderful moment at the end of the story of Samson where the Bible says that Samson's hair begins to grow back. This is significant because it shows the grace of God in Samson's life. As his hair grows, it is like God is saying, "I forgive you. Here is a second chance.' And what does Samson do with his second chance? He is sure to follow the leadership of the Lord.

With his second chance at life, Samson chooses death. Specifically, Samson chooses to die to Save God's people. He pulls down the central pillars of the enemies' building and causes the entire facility to crumble in on itself. Samson loses his life, but he also takes the lives of many enemies. It was because of Sampson's sacrifice that God's people were ultimately delivered.

This story reminds me so much of our Lord and Savior, Jesus Christ. The way that he delivered his people was by sacrificing himself as well. Except in the event of Jesus's death, he was the only one who died. He did not take down the enemy with him. Instead, his death was what was needed in order to save the enemy. The ones who were crucifying him were given the chance of salvation because he died.

The concept of sacrifice is written all throughout the Bible. There is a whole book that is dedicated to explaining how God's people ought to offer sacrifices. Jesus is the central sacrifice of scripture. And Paul tells the church that they ought to offer their lives as living sacrifices to the Lord. He goes on to say that this is our spiritual act of worship.

And so, I must ask you as you read this Bible study, what have you sacrificed for the Lord recently? There are three things that you can offer to him on any given day. You have time, treasure, and talent. I urge you to make the decision today to offer him all three, for this is your spiritual act of worship.

REFLECTION

Day 1: Why is sacrifice central to the Bible?

Day 2: What do we learn about God when Samson's hair grows back?

Day 3: What time can you sacrifice to God?

Day 4: What talent can you sacrifice to God?

Day 5: What treasure can you sacrifice to God?

Day 6: How is sacrifice an act of worship?

Day 7: Write a letter of promise to God about what you're willing to give to Him.

PRAYER REQUESTS

ANSWERED PRAYERS

Week 23
Boaz - Redeemer

"I know that my redeemer lives,
and that in the end he will stand on the earth."
Job 19:25

Read Ruth 1-4

Do you have a favorite love story? There are hundreds, if not thousands, of them that have been produced over the years. Some are written down in books. Others have been made into movies. I am sure by now that you have plenty that are in podcast form. If you have not yet read the story of Ruth, then you are missing out on one of the greatest love stories in the Bible.

Once again, since this is a Bible study focused on the men of scripture, we are going to try to understand the Book of Ruth from the perspective of Boaz. Boaz was a businessman in an agricultural society. He had fields of wheat, barley, and grain. These fields were his livelihood. We can infer from scripture that Boaz was a successful man. He had people working for him, and he had products that he was able to spare for the poor.

This is where Ruth comes into the picture. Through an adventure of her own, she found herself in Boaz's field, gleaning some of the leftovers of his crop. Boaz quickly took affection towards her and began to watch out for her. At the end of the story, Boaz and Ruth get married. But they have to go through a process called redemption.

According to the Old Testament law, in order for the widow, Ruth, to be married, she had to find a kinsman redeemer. And the first kinsman redeemer in line was not Boaz. So, Boaz had to find the person who was first in line and ask for his blessing in order to marry Ruth. Boaz goes through all of that trouble and makes the deal he has to make in order to marry the love of his life, Ruth.

The reason this is called a Redemption process is because there is a literal price to be paid along the way. In biblical times, anytime someone was married, the husband's family would pay a price to the bride's family for her hand in marriage. When Boaz paid the price for Ruth, that was what was going on.

This wonderful love story points us forward to the Redemption price that Jesus would pay for his people. We were all in debt to God. Because of our sin, we had a price to pay. And the Bible is clear that that price was our very lives. The Bible says that the wages of sin is death. So, when Jesus went to the cross and died, he was paying the price for us. He is our Redeemer. And he redeemed us because he loved us just like Boaz loved Ruth.

Is there someone on whom you can make this kind of impact? I am not asking you to get married, nor am I asking you to be crucified on an old rugged cross. But I am asking you to look at your life and see if there is someone for whom you can pay the price. They may have a financial need or a physical need. Is there a way that you can redeem the situation and be the hands and feet of Jesus for them?

REFLECTION

Day 1: What does Boaz teach us about the love of God?

Day 2: How does redemption point us to Jesus?

Day 3: Who in your life can you be like Jesus to?

Day 4: How would you pay the price for them?

Day 5: In what ways, outside of money, can you pay the price for another person?

Day 6: What does it mean that Jesus paid the price for us?

Day 7: How does it change your view of salvation to know that your soul cost His life?

PRAYER REQUESTS

ANSWERED PRAYERS

Week 24

Saul - Pride

"When pride comes, then comes disgrace,
but with humility comes wisdom."
PROVERBS 11:2

Read 1 Samuel 9-15

The people of God did not like how God was leading them. They grumbled in the wilderness as Moses led them to the promised land. They pushed back on Joshua's leadership to take the land. Over and over again, God's people fight the leadership that he provides. And that cycle continues as they reject the judges as their leaders.

God's people looked around at the Nations that surrounded them and saw that they were the only nation without a king. This upset them. And so, they cried out to God, asking him for a king. God made it clear to them that he was their king. They did not need another. But they persisted in their arrogance and demanded that he give them one.

God warned them about this decision and told them that if they were to get a king, they would gain all of the troubles that come with a king. This did not deter them from their desire. And so, God gave them over to their depraved mind. He gave them the king that they wanted. That man's name was Saul.

Saul started out as a good king. He was obedient to the Lord, and He protected his people. But it did not take long for Saul to become a man of pride and arrogance. Throughout the story of Saul, he becomes more and more impressed with himself. And he becomes more and more angry when someone tries to take the glory away from him.

This will be the driving factor behind his determination to eliminate David. You can read more about that in 1 Samuel.

Pride is a destroyer. It ruins lives and reputations. Pride will whisper in your ear that if you do these things, you will come out on top. All the while, it takes a knife and drives it into your back. Pride is deceptive, and it promises things that it cannot keep. This is why the Book of Proverbs tells us that pride comes before the fall. And this was certainly true in Saul's life.

So, take heed, my brother, that pride will not overcome you. Take the posture of Jesus instead of Saul. Jesus was a man of humility. The Bible says that Jesus humbled himself to the point of death, even death on the cross. The God Who resided in glory gave up his right to remain there and descended to earth. He took on a frail human body and lived among sinful people. If you want to see humility over pride, you need to look no further than the cross at Calvary.

If we emulate the humility of Jesus as opposed to the pride of Saul, it is not destruction that we will find. It is life. A life of humility is how life works best, according to the Bible. And so, let's pursue that kind of life. Let's deny the example of Saul. Let us be men who put others first. And more than anything, let us be men who put God first.

REFLECTION

Day 1: What would you say is the definition of pride?

Day 2: Why is pride so destructive?

Day 3: What makes humility a hard path to follow?

Day 4: In what ways was Saul prideful?

Day 5: In what ways do you tend to be prideful?

Day 6: Has God ever humbled you? If so, how?

Day 7: What can you do this week in an act of humility?

PRAYER REQUESTS

ANSWERED PRAYERS

Week 25

Jonathan - Friendship

"As iron sharpens iron, so one person sharpens another."
Proverbs 27:17

Read 1 Samuel 18-20

Who is your best friend? And what made that person your best friend? It is interesting that when you are younger, best friends come and go very quickly. And there aren't many criteria for them to be your best friend. It may simply be that they sat beside you in school and so they were your best friend.

But as you get older, your standards for friendship rise significantly. And for someone to be your best friend, they have to be a pretty special person. In the life of David and Jonathan, their friendship was unique in a lot of ways. The most striking way is that Jonathan's dad was often trying to kill David. Can you imagine existing in a friendship like that?

And yet Jonathan was faithful to David. Because of their friendship, Jonathan defended David's life. Jonathan even helped David to escape one of the traps of King Saul. You could very easily say that Jonathan and David were best friends. And one of the markers of that friendship was loyalty.

One of the markers of any good friendship or relationship is one of loyalty. Loyalty is the concept of having someone's back. It means that you are always going to be on their side. You may contradict them and push back against them, but at the end of the day, you are still on their side. Jonathan was always on the side of David. Even when that meant he had to side against his own father. What a special friendship that must have been.

We are called to be friends like Jonathan and David. We are supposed to put our Brothers and Sisters in Christ first. We are to be loyal to one another. We are to assume the best of one another. And we are to help one another in their times of need. Christians ought to be the best of friends. The very values of Christ make that to be true.

What kind of friend are you? I hope you will tell me that you are a true friend who is true. I hope that you will say to me that you are a reliable friend. I hope that you will honestly be able to report that you are a friend in the good times and the bad alike. This is what the Bible would have you to be.

And the gospel would compel you to take it one step further. The good news of Jesus's forgiveness and mercy to all who believe in him pushes us to offer forgiveness and mercy to others. It calls us to be a friend to those who are not a friend to us. What a challenge this is. But the news is still. We have a great savior to help us meet this great challenge. And so, brother, be a friend today.

REFLECTION

Day 1: Why is your best friend your best friend?

Day 2: What does it mean to be a good friend?

Day 3: Why should Christians be very good friends?

Day 4: Does this mean that we should not be friends with non-Christians?

Day 5: Are there other notable friendships in scripture?

Day 6: In what ways have you struggled to be a good friend recently?

Day 7: What can you do this week to be a better friend?

PRAYER REQUESTS

ANSWERED PRAYERS

Week 26

David - Slipped

"For all have sinned and fall short of the glory of God."
Romans 3:23

Read 2 Samuel 11-12

King David is highly known as the greatest king of Israel. There is simply no dispute over the matter. His prestige is unmatched. He was called the man after God's own heart. He was the good and righteous king who would replace the wicked and prideful King Saul. All of the New Testament refers back to King David and his lineage, even though King Saul was the first.

The compliments you could pay to King David are simply endless. He was a great warrior. He was a wise leader. He was well-liked and loved by his followers. He was able to rally unlikely men together to accomplish impossible goals. The list could go on and on.

But King David was not a perfect man. There are no perfect men. The blemish on David's life is far more than a small stain. There is blood on his hands. As you read about the adulterous choices of King David and Bathsheba, you will see that his sin results in the murder of an innocent man.

I draw this to your attention, brother, so as not to condemn King David. That is not my job, nor is it yours. That is the responsibility of God himself. I want you to see this moment in King David's life to remind you that you are not perfect either. Your life may be going well, and you may feel very faithful to God. If that is true, then praise His holy name. But it is only by his grace that you are able to say so.

In David's weak moment, he was far from the grace of God. In that moment, he denied his need for God and his word, and he plunged himself into the depths of his deepest desire. And the further down the rabbit trail he went, the worse things got.

Friend, I want you to read this as a reminder to yourself and a warning. There is no one who is good, no not one. We are all in daily, even hourly, need for the grace of God. This ought to change how we pray to our Father. Instead of simply praying in the morning and in the evening and occasionally at meals, we ought to be ever in prayer. Because we are ever in need of the grace of God.

Take some time today to consider just how different your life would be if you did not know Jesus. Then, consider the fact that the only reason you know who Jesus is so, because God graciously sent a messenger to you. That messenger may have been your family, your church, or a stranger on the street. Nevertheless, it was God's hand at work in their lives that allowed them to hear the good news. Do not for a moment think that you don't need the grace of God today.

REFLECTION

Day 1: Why do you think King David made this mistake?

Day 2: How did things get out of hand so quickly for him?

Day 3: What does David's life teach us about sin?

Day 4: What are your sin struggles?

Day 5: What are you doing to fight against those sin struggles?

Day 6: Who told you the good news of Jesus?

Day 7: Write a letter to that person thanking them for being the grace of God to you.

PRAYER REQUESTS

ANSWERED PRAYERS

WEEK 27
SOLOMON - WISDOM

"If any of you lacks wisdom, you should ask God,
who gives generously to all without finding fault,
and it will be given to you "
JAMES 1:5

Read 1 Kings 3-4

Who is the wisest person that you know? It may be your father or grandmother. But who is it that you go to when you need advice? If we were able, many of us would go to Solomon for all of our advice. He is renowned as the wisest man in the bible. Much of the wisdom literature that we have in the Old Testament was written by him. In the passages of Scripture that you are reading this week, you will see why that is the case.

When given the chance to ask God for anything, Solomon chose to ask for wisdom. I am not sure that this is what we would have asked for. Perhaps you would have asked for money or fame. But Solomon asks for wisdom. And that is, in fact, a wise thing to ask for. You see, it is through wisdom that you can gain money and fame. And so, God blessed Solomon not only for asking for wisdom but also blessed him with money and fame.

The Book of Proverbs is probably Solomon's most famous work. Within its pages, you will read all kinds of wise and sometimes pithy sayings from Solomon. However, an overlooked wisdom writing from Solomon is the Book of Ecclesiastes. In this sobering book, you will read that wisdom, money, and fame were not satisfying to Solomon's soul.

The more you learn about King Solomon, the more you will realize that while he had everything at his fingertips, he was never quite happy. He expresses this frustration and sorrow in the book of Ecclesiastes. The irony of Solomon's life is that he had the wisdom of God but was not able to use that wisdom to follow God. It is only through following the Lord that Solomon could have been content with what he had.

If we are to be men of God, we need to be two things. We need to be both wise and content. These two things go hand in hand. Wisdom will tell you that you need to be content. Had Solomon heeded his own advice from The Book of Proverbs, he may have realized this. What can you do today to be a wise and content man?

I would suggest to you that wisdom begins with listening. Maybe you need to spend even more time reading God's word and listening to what he has to say. Maybe you need to reach out to someone and ask for advice on a situation that you are going through. Maybe you just need to spend more time with an older man or woman of God who can pour into your life.

And when those nuggets of wisdom come from various sources, you will find them contentment is what you have to strive for afterward. We can sometimes think that wisdom is this Shining Light moment where everything finally makes sense. But in the end, wisdom gives us answers we have known for a long time and helps us to come to terms with them. In that process, we find contentment.

REFLECTION

Day 1: Who is the wisest person you know?

Day 2: How would you define wisdom?

Day 3: When is a time that you needed wisdom?

Day 4: When is a time that God gave you wisdom in a hard situation?

Day 5: When we lack wisdom, what are we supposed to do?

Day 6: How can we share our wisdom with other people?

Day 7: Is there someone who needs a wise word in your life?

PRAYER REQUESTS

ANSWERED PRAYERS

Week 28
Rehoboam - Foolish

"Listen to advice and accept discipline,
and at the end you will be counted among the wise."
Proverbs 19:20

Read 1 Kings 11-12

If Solomon is the wisest King to have ever reigned in Israel, then it is probably safe to say that his son Rehoboam was the most foolish King ever to reign in Israel. Where Solomon heated the advice of others his son was not willing to do so. And his lack of willingness to listen to the elders who would give him counsel put him in a lot of trouble.

As the story unfolds, you will see that this cost him not only his kingdom but it cost him the entire kingdom. The nation of Israel was split into two because of the foolishness of this one king. Where there once was one United Kingdom called Israel, there would now be a northern kingdom and a southern kingdom. The northern kingdom still bears the name of Israel. And the southern Kingdom now bears the name Judah.

Let this story be a cautionary tale for you, dear brother. There are going to be moments in your life the way you receive advice from an older person. That advice may not seem right to you at the moment. But even so, take extra caution if you reject the advice given to you by an elder. It could very well be that that elder knows the path you are about to go down because they themselves have been down it already.

For example, if you are dating someone and some of the older members of your family are unsure of whether or not it is a good idea for you to be in a relationship with that person, be warned. Or, for another instance, think about a career change. If someone who is older and wiser in your life advises you against a career change, be warned. Even if that career change would bring you more financial flexibility, it may not be the wisest decision in the end.

There are plenty of ways that you may receive advice that goes against your natural instinct. But let's be honest. Our gut instinct is not always the best one. Heed the advice of the older men and women of God who are in your life. Be sensitive to the Holy Spirit and how He speaks to you through them and through God's word. Do not be hasty in your decision-making.

My grandpa had a piece of advice that has been faithful and true through the years. He would tell me that before making any big decision, I take a nap. Sleep on it. This time of sleep and rest would give me an opportunity to filter through any emotions that are affecting my judgment on the decision. It would give me time to think and reflect. More than anything, it would give me time to consider the advice of others.

I want to commend you for the advice that was given to me many years ago. If you're facing an important decision, then sleep on it. Take time to consider God's word and God's people. Do not reject the advice just because it doesn't seem right to you.

REFLECTION

Day 1: Can you think of a time that you have rejected advice from someone?

Day 2: Why did you reject advice in that situation?

Day 3: Would things have turned out differently if you had listened to the advice you were given?

Day 4: Is there a time when someone rejected your advice?

Day 5: How did things work out for them?

Day 6: How insistent should we be when giving advice?

Day 7: In what way should you respond to someone who refused to take advice?

PRAYER REQUESTS

ANSWERED PRAYERS

Week 29
Jeroboam - Usurper

"The integrity of the upright guides them,
but the unfaithful are destroyed by their duplicity."
Proverbs 11:3

Read 1 Kings 12-14

Just as God predicted, there was trouble in paradise. If you know the story of how Saul came to be the first king of Israel, then you know that God warned them about getting a king to begin with. God was to be their King, and that was supposed to be enough for them. But the people complained, and God gave them over to their foolish demands.

However, God was faithful in warning them that if they made this decision to get a king, there would be trouble ahead. Well, now trouble has found them. The kingdom is now divided. They are only four generations into the life of the nation, and it is all falling apart.

One of the main contributors to the downfall of the nation of Israel is a man by the name of Jeroboam. He was a troublemaker, to put it lightly. To put it in more biblical terms, he was a usurper of authority. He did not like how the kingdom was being run, and he decided that he would take a shot at the throne. He and the son of Solomon became enemies quickly.

The way that Jeroboam sought to take the throne from the rightful king was by gaining an alliance with the enemies of God's people. I guess it is true that the enemy of my enemy is my friend. Even if that enemy is your own personal enemy. Jeroboam sought the help of foreign nations who had long been enemies of Israel in order to overthrow and take the throne of Israel.

Jeroboam was a manipulator. He was willing to use whoever, whenever, to get whatever he wanted. He would scheme, plan, and plot his way toward his goal. I can imagine that Jeroboam was the type of man that everyone was drawn to. He probably had a silver tongue of sorts. But at the end of the day, he was not a man that could be trusted.

Some of you reading this book may be very good with your words. You might be the kind of person that could talk your way out of any situation. I want to warn you of the power that comes with that ability. The ability to convince and persuade people to follow you is an Incredible Gift but can be used for incredible pain.

If God has gifted you with the ability to lead people and influence people, I want to encourage you to use that solely for his glory. Sometimes, this means that it is not for your own glory. Maybe the way God wants you to lead people is to see him. I am lifted up. And for you to have no real following or authority. This can be a hard path to follow, but whatever God has for your life is the best thing for you.

REFLECTION

Day 1: Would you consider yourself a natural leader?

Day 2: What qualities do you possess that make you a leader or a follower?

Day 3: Would you agree that everyone is leading someone in their lives?

Day 4: Who might you be leading?

Day 5: What kind of example are you setting for them?

Day 6: If you set a good example, could you say that you set a gospel example?

Day 7: What needs to change so you can set a gospel example for those who follow you?

PRAYER REQUESTS

ANSWERED PRAYERS

Week 30
Josiah - Reformer

"Do your best to present yourself to God as one approved, a worker who does not need to be ashamed and who correctly handles the word of truth."
2 Timothy 2:15

Read 2 Kings 22-23

When I was a youth pastor in North Carolina, I took a mission trip to Montana. On that mission trip, we had a family with five kids and join us. One of the children's name was Josiah. He was a blonde-headed little boy who was about 4 years old. He quickly became my buddy on that trip.

A lot of the work that was done on this mission trip was construction-related. So, you can imagine that there was not much that Josiah was able to do. But he stuck by my side, and we swung hammers at nails. The wood that held those nails wasn't really attached to anything, and we weren't accomplishing much, but he was having a great time.

Every time that I read the story of Josiah in Second Kings, I think of my little buddy on that mission trip. The King Josiah was only 8 years old when he took the throne. And yet, it was under his leadership that the greatest reformation in the history of Israel took place. And Josiah's steps toward the reformation were rather simple.

You see, there came a day when an old book was found in the city. That old book happened to be the word of God. Josiah had that book read to him, and he took in every word. With his childlike faith, he simply believed and followed what God's word said to do. And in following God's word, he led the nation of Israel back to where they should have been all along.

Oh, how simple it is to find a reformation if you know what to look for. And it is a simple thing to look for. If we want to be more like what God would have us to be, we simply need to find God's word. And we have God's word in the Bible. The book that you are reading week to week is literally God's word to his people.

Although the Bible was originally written many years ago, it is still very relevant to God's people today. All of the principles that it contains are ones that can be applied to your life. It is a book that was meant to span centuries and still speak to the hearts of God's people. And it can still speak to your heart today.

I want to encourage you today to be a man of the word. To take the posture of King Josiah and read it regularly. Take it at face value and trust it. Seek to follow it with every fiber of your being. When you do this, you will experience a great reformation in your own heart and life. You will find yourself following more closely with Jesus than ever before.

This is the type of king that God wanted in Israel. And this is the type of man that God wants for you to be today. A man of the word. A man who seeks to know what it says and to follow it with all of his heart.

REFLECTION

Day 1: Do you know anyone who is wise beyond their years?

Day 2: Why do you think they are that way?

Day 3: Why did God's word spark a revival in Israel?

Day 4: In what areas do you need to go back to God's Word?

Day 5: How does your local church need to go back to God's Word?

Day 6: What does revival look like to you?

Day 7: When have you experienced revival?

PRAYER REQUESTS

ANSWERED PRAYERS

Week 31

Elijah - Prayer

"Rejoice always, pray continually, give thanks in all circumstances; for this is God's will for you in Christ Jesus. "
1 Thessalonians 5:16-18

Read 1 Kings 17-19

There are men and women who pray in ways that seem far more powerful than my own. Have you experienced this? It seems like they have a connection with God that is stronger and more tangible than mine. I know that when they pray, the Lord hears them in a special way.

One such person in Scripture was Elijah. He is known for a lot of things. He was a miracle worker. He was a faithful prophet. But all of this was steeped in an intense and powerful relationship with God. God would speak to Elijah, and Elijah would respond. They would talk with each other in a way that is hard to even imagine.

The highlight of Elijah's prayer ministry was on Mount Carmel. He called out to God to rain fire down from Heaven. This was not for personal gain but for the sake of God's holy name, that he prayed. When fire rained down from Heaven to consume the offering that was presented at the altar Elijah had built, God made it known that He alone was the one true God. Elijah prayed in light of the glory of God.

Jesus prayed this way, too. You can read about it in John 17. Jesus prays for the Father to be glorified in all that He did. Jesus even prayed that He would be glorified for the sake of the great name of the Father. As you learn more about the role of the Holy Spirit, you'll learn that His purpose is to highlight and bring glory to the Son and the Father.

If this is how Elijah prayed and this is how Jesus prayed, shouldn't this be what characterizes our prayers? This does not mean that we don't ask God for things. We absolutely do. Elijah did, and so did the Christ. But when we come to God with prayers that seek for something, we must do it with the glory of God in mind.

Perhaps our prayers out to switch from, "Dear God, let me get that promotion," to "Dear God, I want to bring glory to Your name. If you allow me the promotion, I will glorify you. If you don't, I will glorify you still. Your will be done, and Your kingdom come on earth as it is in Heaven." This type of prayer takes a dramatic shift in our hearts. It requires us to put ourselves second to Almighty God.

Take some time this week to evaluate your prayer life. What prompts most of your prayers? How often are you praying in light of the glory of God? After you've spent time looking over these things, make whatever necessary changes come to light. As our brother James says, referencing Elijah, "Therefore confess your sins to each other and pray for each other so that you may be healed. The prayer of a righteous person is powerful and effective."

REFLECTION

Day 1: What is your prayer life like?

Day 2: What can you do to strengthen your prayer life?

Day 3: Who can you learn about prayer from?

Day 4: What do you need to spend extra time praying about this week?

Day 5: Who can you offer to pray for?

Day 6: What did that person ask you to pray for?

Day 7: How did God answer that prayer this week?

PRAYER REQUESTS

ANSWERED PRAYERS

Week 32
Elisha - Follower

"Then he said to them all: "Whoever wants to be my disciple must deny themselves and take up their cross daily and follow me. "
Luke 9:23

Read 2 Kings 2-4

Elijah had a successor in his ministry. Before being taken to Heaven in a chariot of fire, Elijah had passed the prophetic torch to his faithful follower, Elisha. I've always been intrigued by the similarities of their names, but no reason is given for that in Scripture. It would not benefit us to make speculations.

What is clear in Scripture is that Elisha was given a weighty task. He was to follow the famous Elijah in ministry. He was supposed to be the new voice of God to the wayward Israelite nation. Elisha knew what kind of pressure would come with this responsibility, and so he asked his teacher for a double portion of the blessing that he had received.

As you will read, Elisha's ministry thrived in many of the ways Elijah's had. It was clear that he would be able to bear the burden and speak the word of the Lord to His people. There are a lot of things we could learn from Elisha's life, but I want us to focus this week on the relationship between him and Elijah.

Elisha was like a mentor or apprentice to Elijah. He shadowed him for much of his ministry. He got to see him on the good days and the bad. He was there when Elijah had a fresh word from the Lord and when there had been silence for days and days. Elisha got to see first-hand what it meant to be a prophet long before he ever became one.

When you go to the New Testament, this type of relationship is described in a new way. It is called make disciples. This is the Great Commission and last command of Jesus before He ascended into Heaven. He said, "Therefore go and make disciples of all nations, baptizing them in the name of the Father and of the Son and of the Holy Spirit, and teaching them to obey everything I have commanded you. And surely, I am with you always, to the very end of the age."

Every man of God is to be a disciple and a disciple-maker. We are all to be learning from someone in the faith and seeking to teach another. This sounds more daunting than it really is. A disciple is not an expert or a professional theologian. You do not have to be a pastor to be a disciple-maker. A disciple is simply a follower. That's what the word means. If you follow Jesus, you're a disciple of His. Therefore, any way that you can help someone else follow Jesus is by making disciples.

If you can offer encouragement or correction to a brother, you're helping to make disciples. If you can teach someone what you've been taught, you're making disciples. If you can pray with someone when they are going through a hard time, you're playing a part in making disciples.

REFLECTION

Day 1: Are you more naturally a leader or a follower?

Day 2: Why do you think of yourself that way?

Day 3: Who in your life do you have to follow?

Day 4: Who in your life do you choose to follow?

Day 5: Is there anyone you want to follow more closely?

Day 6: why do you want to follow them more closely?

Day 7: What does it mean to be a follower or someone else?

PRAYER REQUESTS

ANSWERED PRAYERS

WEEK 33

JONAH - RUNNING FROM GOD

"Trust in the Lord with all your heart and lean not on your own understanding; in all your ways submit to him, and he will make your paths straight."
PROVERBS 3:5-6

Read Jonah 1-4

Have you ever been asked to do something that you really didn't want to do? I can remember that, as a kid, one of the things that I detested doing was brushing my teeth. I know it seems silly and trivial now, but at the time, it seemed like the world's worst torture. So, what I would do to get out of brushing my teeth is go into the bathroom when my parents ask me to brush my teeth. I would turn on the water, and I would even stick my toothbrush under the water to make sure that it got wet. So that when my parents checked the toothbrush, they would know that I had "brushed my teeth. "

As a kid, I thought I was very clever in coming up with this ingenious plan. But as a parent now, I realize that I probably wasn't really getting away with anything. I'm sure my parents were very well aware of my poor dental habits. In the story of JOANNE, we have a similar type of silliness. God gives Jonah a command to follow. He tells him to go and preach the news of repentance to the city of Ninevah. But Jonah does not want to do that. He has many reasons for deeply disliking the people of them. And so, he tries to do the silliest thing imaginable. He tries to run from God.

It would be worth your time to take a moment to consider just how foolish of an objective that would be. God is an all-powerful, all-knowing, and ever-present being in this World. He would be literally impossible to run from. And yet, this is exactly what Jonah chooses to do in his childish response to God's call on his life.

But it is impossible to run from God. And because God loves you so deeply that he will not let you run forever. God caught Jonah in the belly of a large fish. Friend, can I point out to you that no matter how much running you may do from God? God will eventually catch you. And he probably won't gently and lovingly catch you in his arms. It probably will stink a lot like it does in the belly of a large fish. But praise be to God that when he catches us and puts us through a disciplinary process, it is with love in mind. It is so that we would return to his loving arms.

Jonah wrestles, even after being caught and delivered out of the belly of the large fish. He still struggles to do what God called him to do. And yet God continues to push him forward to accomplish his mission. This shows us that God is relentless in getting his will done. He will not stop until what he wants done is done. And so, it only is a frustration to ourselves when we run from him. It's only a frustration to ourselves when we come up with excuses to not serve him. Our lives would be simpler if we would simply do what the Lord asks us to do. This does not mean that our lives will be easier or pain-free. Preaching the message of repentance to a hateful nation was not an easy job. But it is simple. Do what the Lord requires, and He will carry you through.

REFLECTION

Day 1: Why did Jonah run from God?

Day 2: Why didn't Jonah's knowledge of God stop him from acting that way?

Day 3: Have you ever tried running from a responsibility?

Day 4: How did that run turn out?

Day 5: What are the benefits of doing what God says first?

Day 6: How does our delayed obedience hurt others?

Day 7: What was the lesson from Jonah that stood out to you?

PRAYER REQUESTS

ANSWERED PRAYERS

Week 34

Shadrach, Meshack, Abednego - Even If

"The fear of the Lord is the beginning of wisdom, and knowledge of the Holy One is understanding. "
Proverbs 9:10

Read Daniel 1-3

There are very few people in my life that I would call fearless. It's hard to find someone who seems as if they have nothing to fear. And if you really think about it, fearlessness isn't really a thing. Everybody struggles with fear. Everyone is afraid of something. But what looks like fearlessness is really not allowing fear to stop you from action.

That is the type of fearlessness that we find in the story of Shadrach, Meshach, and Abednego. These men appear to be completely without fear. But that is not entirely the case. I am sure that they feared death. I am sure that they feared the pain and the punishment that would ensue when they were disobedient to the king. But they happened to have a greater fear than the king or death itself. They feared the Lord God.

That fear was not one that kept them on their knees trembling. It was a fear that brought them to their knees humbly in prayer. They so feared, revered, and trusted God that they would face anything else because of it. They loved and trusted the king of heaven so much that they had no fear of the king of this earth.

The lifestyle that they lived, in the stance that they took, was a witness to those around them. The way that they lived was a message. Their actions spoke just as loudly as their words.

And let's be sure to note that they had some very loud words. They essentially said to the king that even if they were to die for their belief, they would never bow to the king. That is a loud statement coming from a slave and a foreign nation.

And it is fair to say that their actions spoke louder. They stood when everyone else bowled. They willingly were tied and tossed into the fiery furnace. And as the flames singed and scorched and destroyed the ropes that bound them, they stood unarmed. So incredible were their actions, and so miraculous was the action of their God that the king Counted what he had said before. He saw the majesty and power of the one true god of the Bible. In other words, he now had a fear greater than any other. He began to fear the Lord.

Friend, as you read this passage this week, I want you to ask yourself the question: do you fear the Lord? Is he the one thing that drives all other things in your life? Or is there something that you fear more than him? Ask yourself why that fear exists. And seek to root it out of your life.

REFLECTION

Day 1: Do you know of anyone who was in a life-or-death situation?

Day 2: How do you think you would handle that?

Day 3: Is there anything someone could threaten to make you turn your back on God?

Day 4: Would God still be good if he let the three men die in the furnace?

Day 5: Why was there a fourth man in the fire?

Day 6: Do you think the king's new decree was genuine?

Day 7: How do you think the three men were different after that day?

PRAYER REQUESTS

ANSWERED PRAYERS

Week 35
Daniel - Visions

"In the last days, God says, I will pour out my Spirit on all people. Your sons and daughters will prophesy, your young men will see visions, your old men will dream dreams."
Acts 2:17

Read Daniel 7-10

I have had some pretty bizarre dreams in my life. Even last night, I had a dream that I was smoking a cigarette for some reason. To be clear, I am not a smoker. I have not smoked anything in my entire life. And yet, that was the subject of my dream last night. I was frantically searching for a lighter in order to take a long drag from a cigarette. I'm not even sure why or how my mind came up with that scenario, and yet, that is what I was living in.

No matter how crazy or bizarre. Our dreams may seem nothing will compare to the dreams and visions that Danielle saw. As you read these chapters, you will begin to get a sense of the incomprehensibility of our God. In God 's goodness and kindness, he gives interpretations to Daniel along the way. So, we are not left without any hope. But nonetheless, it is still very confusing to read. Take your time, and do not get hung up on details that you don't quite get. Look for the big picture.

If you're looking for the big picture, you will find one called the Ancient of Days and one called the Son of Man. These are the two most important characters that you can recognize in these passages. The ancient of days is another name for God, the Father. He is the Ancient One who has been around before days even began. He is the one calling the shots and giving the directives.

The second person known as the Son of Man is, in fact, Jesus. He is the king of God's people. He is the one who will reign forever and ever under the leadership of the Ancient of Days. In the midst of all the craziness of this story, even the visions of Daniel point us to Jesus.

When reading stories about men and women who have incredible visions, we can be tempted to try to dissect and understand our own visions and dreams. But let us be very careful in this. Because I had a dream about smoking last night, this does not mean that the Lord wants me to take up the habit. In fact, I would say the overwhelming majority of dreams that are dreamed by anyone are just simply dreams.

But God has occasionally, in select a few cases, spoken through dreams and visions to his people. This type of revelation seems to have effectively ceased in our day. It would not be fair to say that they are completely gone because our God can do whatever he wants to do. But our primary form of communication with God and our primary understanding of his revelation is simply his word. And so yes, marvel at the dreams and the visions that you see in scripture, but do not put much weight in stock on your own.

REFLECTION

Day 1: Have you ever had a vivid dream you couldn't forget?

Day 2: Why do you think God spoke to Daniel through dreams?

Day 3: Why do you think God doesn't do that very often anymore?

Day 4: When you're unsure of something in your life, where can you go for help?

Day 5: What about Daniel's dream stood out to you?

Day 6: What questions do you need to do more research about?

Day 7: How do the visions help us understand more about Jesus?

PRAYER REQUESTS

ANSWERED PRAYERS

WEEK 36
JOSEPH - FAITHFUL HUSBAND

"Husbands, love your wives, just as Christ loved the church and gave himself up for her."
EPHESIANS 5:25

Read Matthew 1-2

I recently preached a sermon series on the first few chapters of the book of Matthew. It is interesting how Matthew highlights Joseph's experience instead of Mary's. Luke highlights Mary in his gospel account. As I was studying the book, I found myself having a really hard time putting myself into Joseph's shoes. Who could really imagine all of the complex emotions that would come with that scenario?

But there is one sad thing about Joseph that stuck out with me while I was studying. He is called a righteous man. And that is truly the right word. What else would you use to describe a man who goes through all the heat went through, and still remains faithful to Mary? Not only does he remain faithful to her, but even if there is a hint of adultery, he is willing to silently and secretly end the relationship. I know that if I had been cheated on in that type of scenario. I would've been ready to throw in the towel altogether and make a big fuss about it.

I can remember a time when I was Gelan and the pain that came with that. I did not want to speak to that person ever again, let alone hear from them, but they were carrying the Messiah. The integrity and maturity that had to exist within Joseph is hard to put into words. And so, I guess the best way to describe it would be that he was simply a righteous man.

In light of that, I've been asking myself, and I encourage you to ask yourself, how would you be described by the Lord? Would he be able to rightly call you a righteous man? If not, what other words would he use to describe you? Maybe you're better described as a prideful or jealous man. Maybe other people would call you a lazy or self-centered man.

Whatever reputation you have earned for yourself, I want you to know that it does not have to stay forever. The power of the gospel and the redeeming message of Jesus is one of life change. At the end of the day, it is one that could change even the most tarnished of reputations to a glorious one. Not so that you would absolve yourself or that you would gain any glory from it. But so that others may see what God has done in your life and come and worship him.

Take time to examine yourself, and ask the Lord to reveal to you your struggles. He was faithful to do it. So, he makes that plane. Ask him to search your heart and show you its sinister depths. And then give those things as quickly as you can to the Lord to handle. Strive to be a righteous man by the grace of God.

REFLECTION

Day 1: Have you ever been cheated on?

Day 2: Would you be able to forgive someone who cheated on you?

Day 3: What would you have done if you were in Joseph's place?

Day 4: What convicted Joseph of the truth?

Day 5: Have you ever been in a situation when you didn't know who to believe?

Day 6: What helped you decide what to believe?

Day 7: How would you respond to an angel appearing to you?

PRAYER REQUESTS

ANSWERED PRAYERS

WEEK 37
ZECHARIAH - MUTE

""For my thoughts are not your thoughts, neither are your ways my ways," declares the Lord. "As the heavens are higher than the earth, so are my ways higher than your ways and my thoughts than your thoughts."
ISAIAH 55:8-9

Read Luke 1

I have friends who could talk to a brick wall. Friends that have never met a stranger and would carry on full-blown conversations with literally anyone in their path. I am not one of those people. I am an introvert through and through. It takes a lot of energy for me to have Conversations with a bunch of people. I often wonder why the Lord gave me the ministry position that he has given me.

I am not sure of Zechariah's disposition, but I am sure of what happened to him. He was mute because of his unbelief of what the Lord was going to do through him and his family. This may have come as a welcome relief at first. Perhaps Zachariah was the type of person to talk nonstop. But I'm sure as its comical nature faded away, its seriousness began to settle in. He would not be allowed to speak until his son was born, and he would bear the name John. This is John the Baptist as we will come to know him.

When I read the story, I am reminded of the book of Galatians, which says that the Lord will not be mocked. It goes on to say that a man will reap what he sows. Zechariah is not the first one to have a mocking attitude in scripture. But he is one of the few that have been made mute because of it. God takes seriously what he plans to do in the world and how he plans to accomplish it. He will not let anyone or anything or any attitude stand in the way. You may be tempted to have a mocking kind of attitude toward God this year. Even this week, you may be drawn to the idea of doing things your way as opposed to doing things God's way. You can rationalize your own desires in your heart by saying that it is more culturally appropriate to think how you think and not how God thinks. You can say that many of the laws and regulations of the Bible are outdated and from ancient times. But none of those things will shield you from the fact that submitting to those ideas is essentially submitting to mocking God.

How foolish we begin to look when we go against the all-wise God. If we are looking to figure out how life works best, why wouldn't we look to the one who created life itself? Let us not mock God by refusing his commands. Let us not wag our finger in his face by saying that our ways are better than his ways. The Bible is playing on the subject. His ways are higher than our way. His thoughts are greater than our thoughts.

And at the end of the day, this is one of the most beautiful that we can hold onto. If his ways are higher, and his thoughts are greater, then we do not have to be and bear the weight of always being right. We do not have to group around in the dark trying to figure out where the light is. We know exactly where it is. Or rather, should I say that we know exactly who it is? He is the source of all truth and wisdom. We simply need to seek him.

REFLECTION

Day 1: What point was God making when He made Zechariah mute?

Day 2: Why did God allow him to speak again when he named John?

Day 3: What encouragement is there to know that God's ways are better than ours?

Day 4: How have you seen this to be true in your life?

Day 5: Who can you remind of this truth this week?

Day 6: How do you think this experience changed Zechariah?

Day 7: What lessons do you think his wife learned in all of this?

PRAYER REQUESTS

ANSWERED PRAYERS

Week 38
Jesus - Son of God

"Jesus answered, "I am the way and the truth and the life. No one comes to the Father except through me.""
John 14:6

Read Luke 2

Unlike any other man of God that we have studied so far in our time together, studying the person of Jesus will be the most special. Because he is truly a man like no other. The Bible is very clear that Jesus was both fully God and fully man. As you will read, it will tell you that he was conceived of the Holy Spirit and born of a virgin woman named Mary. As hard as this is for us to comprehend, it is nonetheless true. As miraculous as that fact, as hard as this is for us to comprehend, it is nonetheless true. As miraculous as that fact may be, there is an even more incredible thing to consider about the person Jesus.

Jesus is a perfect person who forgives imperfect people. When the angels say that the son of David, the Christ, was being born into the world, they are talking about someone who would meet all of the Old Testament prophecies. It is one of the most important prophecies for us to consider about the person. Jesus is Isaiah 53. When you read that chapter, you will see that the coming Christ, the son of David, would be someone who would bear the sins of God's people. Like a sacrificial lamb, he would be killed for their sake.

But the sacrificial lamb had to be a perfect lamb. It had to be spotless. One without any blemish. He had to be blameless. And this is what Jesus accomplished in his life. He was truly righteous in everything that he thought he said or did. And with a perfect righteousness to put on his account before the Father, he took that to the cross. And on the cross, he traded his perfection for our imperfection.

The Bible says that Jesus became sin for those who knew no sin and that we might become the righteousness of God. What that means is that all who would place their faith in the perfect life and sacrificial death of Jesus would be forgiven of their sins and be given the righteousness of the sin one. In the news of Jesus, it just gets better. Not only did he live a perfect life and die a sacrificial death, but he also was resurrected from the grave.

In his resurrection from the grave, Jesus proved that everything he said was true. We can trust that his life was truly perfect. We can know for sure that his death was truly sacrificial. We can know and trust these things because he did not stay in the tomb. God, the father, resurrected him from the dead, almost as if to show that he accepts his payment on the cross.

This week, I do not want to encourage you to try to emulate anything or anyone. I want to simply encourage you to be thankful for Jesus, the son of God. Yes, we ought to try to be like him and think like him, but for this week, would you just rest in the good news of the Gospel? Jesus was perfect, so we no longer have to be.

REFLECTION

Day 1: Why is it important that Jesus is human?

Day 2: Why is it important that Jesus is divine?

Day 3: What would happen if either of those things were not true?

Day 4: When you think about His life, what stands out?

Day 5: If Jesus didn't die on the cross, would you have any hope?

Day 6: What is the significance of His resurrection?

Day 7: Write a prayer of praise to Jesus.

PRAYER REQUESTS

ANSWERED PRAYERS

Week 39
Simeon - Blessed

"Praise be to the God and Father of our Lord Jesus Christ, who has blessed us in the heavenly realms with every spiritual blessing in Christ."
Ephesians 1:3

Luke 2

What is the longest amount of time that you have waited for something? Maybe you waited for your wedding day, or you waited for the chance to get your driver's license. Whatever it was, I doubt you waited longer than Simeon waited for this promise to be fulfilled in his life. Simeon was promised at some point in his life that he would see Christ before he passed away. We don't necessarily know how long ago that was, but the way the story reads leads us to believe that it was for quite some time.

As someone who worked in the temple, Simeon saw thousands, if not millions, of people come through. He met people from all walks of life who were coming to either offer sacrifices or make prayers known to the Lord. It was part of Shehan's job to help people with this process. And so, undoubtedly, he had met so many people and wondered. Would today be the day that I meet the one person I have been longing to meet?

God was faithful in keeping his promise to Simeon, and one day, a woman named Mary brought a little baby boy named Jesus into the presence of Simeon. And upon holding him in his arms, Simeon knew, without any doubt, that this, indeed, was the Christ. Jesus was the one that he had been waiting for so long. And so, Simeon pronounced a blessing over Jesus that was incredibly accurate when you look back at the whole life of Jesus.

The blessing of Jesus that Sammy pronounced said that Jesus would effectively divide the world. When people looked at him and saw his ministry, they would either be all for him or all against him. There was not going to be any middle ground or fence to sit on. And that is certainly true of our Lord and Savior. His followers are all in all out.

This sparks a question in my mind and in my heart. What do you think of when you look at Jesus? When you read of him in the gospels, are you driven to worship him? When you see the prophecies in the Old Testament that point to him, are you drawn to bring him praise? Or do you find yourself bored with Scripture? Maybe you read the word, and the only thing you feel is confused.

I want to encourage you today to spend time in the world looking for Jesus. And when you find him, worship him. This does not mean that you won't face moments of confusion. This does not mean that you won't face seasons where boredom isn't a part of your routine. But regardless of the season you are in, there is always a reason to worship Jesus. It is your duty and your privilege as a Christian to look diligently for those reasons each and every day.

REFLECTION

Day 1: Have you ever waited a long time for something?

Day 2: Was it worth the wait? Why or why not?

Day 3: What emotions do you think Simeon experienced when he held Jesus?

Day 4: Do you think he told Mary about the significance of that moment?

Day 5: What stands out to you about the blessing he gave?

Day 6: How did Jesus fulfill what Simeon said about him?

Day 7: Do you think Mary used that blessing to remind Jesus of His purpose growing up?

PRAYER REQUESTS

ANSWERED PRAYERS

Week 40

James - Brother of Christ

"But in your hearts revere Christ as Lord. Always be prepared to give an answer to everyone who asks you to give the reason for the hope that you have. But do this with gentleness and respect."
1 Peter 3:15

Read James 1-5

This week, as you read the book of James, you will read a unique book from a unique perspective. James is unique in that he focuses a lot on the good works that are required of a believer. This is distinct from other writings because Paul spends much of his time in the New Testament, pushing the idea that we are saved by Grace through Faith alone. Both of these concepts are true for the Christian. We are indeed saved by grace through faith alone. But as one pastor rightly said, Faith that saves never comes alone. It will always be accompanied by good works.

The other thing that makes the book of James unique is the author himself. James is the half-brother of Jesus. And as you study the Bible, you will find that James was not a believer in Jesus for His earthly ministry. He grew up as a skeptic. I can imagine that he grew up somewhat jealous of the attention that Jesus naturally got from his family. And so, it is incredible to see the change of heart that takes place in James's life. He goes from a non-believing skeptic to an author of Scripture. Scripture that puts Jesus as the very son of God and someone worth following.

Can you imagine the challenge of growing up as a brother of Jesus? I think that James felt pressured to live up to the standard that his brother was able to live up to. This, no doubt, has affected his view of God and what it means to follow God. In a negative way, this could have led James to the conclusion that he had to live up to and keep all of the rules of God in order to make God happy. But we know that this is not the case. This is the false teaching of the Pharisees. The only way to please God is by faith in his son Jesus. I wonder when James finally came to that conclusion. Maybe it was after Jesus' resurrection that James finally saw him for what he truly was. Whatever the case may be, James came to Faith and became a significant leader in the Christian church.

Maybe you know someone who is a skeptic or a nonbeliever. What can you do to help change their perspective on Jesus? Maybe they need to consider not only the cross of Christ but also the tomb of Christ. The resurrection is a fact, as it says in First Corinthians 15. If you know someone who is a skeptic, spend time showing them the resurrection of Jesus and see what the Lord will do through his word.

This is part of our calling as believers. We are to be ready to give a reason for the hope that is in us. So, when we are approached by a septic or a nonbeliever, we must be ready to show them why we believe. We must be able to tell them the good news of Jesus. This does not mean that we have to have the most eloquent argument. This does not mean that we have to have all of the answers. But this does mean that we have to be Ready and willing to say what we do know about Jesus and pray that the Holy Spirit will finish the job of saving someone's soul.

REFLECTION

Day 1: What are the challenges of growing up in someone's shadow?

Day 2: Why do you think it was hard for James to believe at first?

Day 3: What do you think changed his mind about Jesus?

Day 4: What about James' book is hard for you to understand?

Day 5: What is the hardest command for you to follow?

Day 6: How can you learn to be quick to listen and slow to speak?

Day 7: Who can you pray for healing for today?

PRAYER REQUESTS

ANSWERED PRAYERS

WEEK 41
JUDE - ZEALOUS

"Walk with the wise and become wise,
for a companion of fools suffers harm."
PROVERBS 13:20

Read Jude

Some of my favorite pastors and preachers are those who are confident about what they believe. It is compelling to listen to someone who is so convicted of a certain truth or idea. There are some men and women who take this position too far and become belligerent towards other beliefs. I don't think that is particularly admirable. But those who hold confidently to what they believe while being gracious when speaking to others are some of those who are role models to me in my life and Ministry.

Jude would've been one of those people. He was adamant about what he believed. And he was forceful as he spoke against false teachers. To be clear, he wasn't calling people false teachers if they disagreed on a secondary-level doctrine. He was calling people false teachers who denied one of the core truths of Christianity. For example, if someone denied that Jesus was God, he would call them a false teacher.

The fire and the passion that Jude writes with as he combats some of the false teachings in his day are encouraging and challenging to me. I need to have the same type of fire and passion when speaking about the truth of God 's word. This means that I need to have firm convictions. The only way to get those firm convictions is to study the Bible thoroughly enough to be 100% sure of where I stand on what it teaches. This takes time, effort, and energy. And it does not happen overnight.

If you are wondering to yourself how you can become someone who is 100% sure about what they believe, then let me tell you. What you're doing right now is a good start. Spending time each day and each week studying God's word is where it all begins. Spending time just opening the word and trying to drink in the truth is the cornerstone of growing in your confidence and knowing what is right and what is wrong.

However, there is a second step that must accompany the first. God has gifted and equipped some men to be teachers and pastors. He has equipped both men and women to be theologians and great thinkers about who God is and what his word says. In order to grow in our confidence about the word, we must sit under someone who is already confident about the word. This means that you need to be involved in a local church. This means that you need to be listening to sermons from your pastors. This means that you need to be invested in small group Bible studies. The Christian life was never meant to be a solo journey. Find a faith community that you can trust and go all in with them so that you can be a fiery opponent to false teaching.

REFLECTION

Day 1: Do you feel confident in what you believe about the Bible?

Day 2: What areas do you not feel confident in?

Day 3: How can you grow in your knowledge of these areas?

Day 4: What book of the Bible do you want to spend more time studying?

Day 5: If someone asked you to tell them the gospel, could you do that?

Day 6: Take time to write down what the gospel is.

Day 7: Why do you think defending your faith is an important skill?

PRAYER REQUESTS

ANSWERED PRAYERS

WEEK 42
PETER - LOUD-MOUTH

"Each of you should use whatever gift you have received to serve others, as faithful stewards of God's grace in its various forms."
1 PETER 4:10

Read 1 Peter 1-5

We all have that friend who is known for sticking their foot in their own mouth. Obviously, I don't mean this literally. I hope you don't actually have a friend who is known for sticking their foot in their mouth. That old phrase means that they are known for saying something and then immediately regretting what they said. You may say that they are a loudmouth or they simply have a big mouth. Peter, the disciple of Jesus and apostle in the church was known for this quality.

Throughout the ministry of Jesus, as he worked with Peter, there were many times when he said something that he instantly regretted. For example, he refused when Jesus tried to wash his feet. Jesus told him that he had to wash his feet as an act of service to him. so, Peter doubled down and said Well, then wash all of me. And Jesus corrected him again. It seems as if Peter could never quite get it right. That is until after Jesus was resurrected.

After the resurrection of Jesus, we see a very different Peter. Yes, he still has the quality of being outspoken and bold. But his zeal has been redirected and honed for one singular truth. He is all about Jesus, his death, and his resurrection. Instead of taking his foot in his mouth, he is opening to the truth of God's word for all to hear.

It is incredible to see just how God uses the natural qualities that Peter has for supernatural purposes. The talents and even some of the quirks that Peter had before giving his life to the Lord God use in his new life with the Lord.

This is oftentimes how our God works with us. Before we love and trust in Jesus, we all possess natural skills and talents. But after we place our faith in him, God can redeem those natural skills and talents for supernatural purposes. One of the obvious ways that this happens is for someone who has musical abilities. They can use those musical abilities to help lead worship and a local church. But let's be honest: not many of us have musical or speaking abilities. So, how does God redeem natural qualities in a typical fashion?

Whether it be plumbing, carpentry work, or even accounting. If you are a godly plumber or a fair accountant, then you are using your natural abilities to display the supernatural character of our God. He can use every skill to bring himself glory. We just have to view our lives in this way. We have to see ourselves as conduits through which the world can see the character of our God. So, as Paul says in the New Testament, everything is hard as unto the Lord.

REFLECTION

Day 1: In what ways do you relate to Peter?

Day 2: What lessons can you learn from his mistakes?

Day 3: How did Peter's life change when he saw that Jesus was resurrected?

Day 4: Why did Jesus make Peter such a foundational person in the early church?

Day 5: What natural qualities do you have?

Day 6: How could those natural qualities be redeemed for the kingdom of God?

Day 7: Are you using your talent and abilities in the local church?

PRAYER REQUESTS

ANSWERED PRAYERS

WEEK 43
PAUL - CHANGED

"Brothers and sisters, I do not consider myself yet to have taken hold of it. But one thing I do: Forgetting what is behind and straining toward what is ahead, I press on toward the goal to win the prize for which God has called me heavenward in Christ Jesus."
PHILIPPIANS 3:13-14

Read Acts 7-9

My testimony is not one full of drama and intrigue. I was raised in a Christian home and went to church every Sunday. If there was ever an event at the church, you knew that my family would be a part of it. And so, when I became a Christian, it was not at all surprising to my friends and to my family. I knew the gospel, and one day. God saved me by the gospel.

The story of Paul is different from my own. Paul was an avid and zealous Jewish person. He would've been one of the Pharisees had he continued on the path that he was going down. If anyone could boast about their own Jewish background and their understanding of the Old Testament, it would've been Paul. So, for him to convert to Christianity was groundbreaking. It was earth-shattering to his friends and to his family. People simply did not understand how he could believe that Jesus actually was the Messiah. And yet, this is exactly what Paul gives his life to.

Like with Peter, God took Paul's natural talents and abilities and used them for supernatural reasons. All of the information and wisdom that he had gained studying the Old Testament for the sake of the Jewish faith. Now, Paul was used to progress the Christian faith.

Because the entire Old Testament simply points us to Jesus. What better knowledge can you have when starting the church?

What I want to point out to Paul is that his change was a lasting change. His love for Jesus and his zeal to preach. The gospel was not a quickly fading love. He spent the rest of his life and even gave up his life for the sake of this mission. Now, I am sure that he faced hard times and questioned things along the way. I'm sure that there were darker seasons and brighter seasons throughout his ministry. But one thing remains true. He did, indeed, finish the race and fight the good fight as a Christian all the way to the end.

I want to encourage my friend to have faith like Paul. Be someone who is going to be all out for Jesus at all times. Consider your life as a race to be run. Do not slow down, and do not give up. Do not throw in the towel for the Lord that you are serving; it is worth every effort. All of the blood that may be spilled. All of the sweat that is sure to be dropped will be worth it.

If you look at the final writings of Paul to Timothy in the books of first and second Timothy, you can hear this kind of satisfaction as he writes. Take this lesson from him. Take this lesson from many of our church fathers and the great saints that have gone before us. In each of their lives, you will find controversy. But you will also find a deep satisfaction in knowing that their life is valuable because they are spending it for the sake of the Savior. Do you want to know that your life has value too? Use it for Jesus. Live all that you have for his sake.

REFLECTION

Day 1: How would you define a testimony?

Day 2: How would you describe the change that Paul experienced?

Day 3: In what ways did your life change when you met Jesus?

Day 4: What is the most dramatic testimony you have ever heard?

Day 5: Have you ever told anybody your own testimony?

Day 6: Why can it be scary to tell someone your testimony?

Day 7: Who can you tell your story to this week?

PRAYER REQUESTS

ANSWERED PRAYERS

WEEK 44
LUKE - DETAILED

"With this in mind, since I myself have carefully investigated everything from the beginning, I too decided to write an orderly account for you, most excellent Theophilus."
LUKE 1:3

Read Luke 22-24

Everybody is wired differently. Some people are big-picture thinkers. They have a hard time focusing on the details and working out the practical points of a plan. But they are great at coming up with the plan. They have wonderful ideas that seem larger than life from time to time. Other people are detail-oriented. They may not come up with the idea, but they definitely can figure out how to make that idea happen. They are focused on the smaller things and the logistics. The same is true of some of our Bible writers. Some of them seem to be bigger-picture-oriented. If you look at our Old Testament profits, many of them carry with them an apocalyptic view of the world. They are thinking about the end more than they seem to be thinking about the right now. With Luke, you get a little bit of the best of both worlds. However, Luke leans toward a detail-oriented person.

When you understand who the person of Luke is, this makes complete sense. Luke is a doctor. You wouldn't want a Doctor Who was not detail-oriented. A big-picture surgeon is one who loses his job quickly because he doesn't know how he is actually going to get the foreign object out of a body. Because Luke is a doctor, he gives us incredible details about the life of Jesus. But perhaps more interesting than anything is that Luke gives the most detailed account of what

Jesus 's body went through when he was beaten by the soldiers and crucified on the cross. It can be excruciating to read. It mirrors what you read about in Isaiah 53. he details for us the brutal treatment that Jesus received. And although this is hard to read, it is good for us to have.

Luke's account of the gospel gives us so much detail that can be historically verified. We can have great faith in the trustworthiness of the entire gospel, according to Luke, because of the accuracy with which he writes. And this can be set of all of the Bible. There are so many details that seem extraneous and unnecessary. The genealogies and the list of numbers can be hard to sift your way through. But they add historical accuracy to the writing of scripture. They give us more and more confidence that what we are reading is, indeed, what happened so long ago.

Sometimes, we think that it is the big-picture visionary people who ought to be leading the church. We can think that detail-oriented people don't have much of a role because they don't tend to have the personalities of the big ideal people. But that simply is not the case. God can and does use all types of people in his church. He needs the visionaries as well as the detail-focused men and women. So, however you find yourself, please know that God can use you and your gifts.

REFLECTION

Day 1: How is Luke's gospel account different from everybody else's?

Day 2: What benefits are there to having a doctor write a section of scripture?

Day 3: Why is historical accuracy important for us?

Day 4: What do you appreciate about Luke's writing style?

Day 5: How does this study change your view of genealogies?

Day 6: Do you know someone who struggles to believe what the Bible says?

Day 7: What can you do to help them believe?

PRAYER REQUESTS

ANSWERED PRAYERS

WEEK 45

MARK - SIMPLE

""The time has come," he said. "The Kingdom of God has come near. Repent and believe the good news!""
MARK 1:15

Read Mark 14-16

I love the gospel, according to Mark. It is fast-paced and action-packed. In my opinion, it is the simplest of the four gospel accounts to understand. You do not need to have a thorough knowledge of Jewish traditions in order to grasp its contents. You do not need to be a great theologian in order to sift through his arguments. It is simply a story of who Jesus was and what he did.

What is so interesting about the book of Mark is really its author. Mark is a relatively nameless person in scripture. We don't read much about him. In fact, we don't know a whole lot about him. But we have discovered, as we have studied the Bible, that Mark was Peter's close friend. If Peter were to have written a gospel account, it would've sounded a lot like Marks. When you read the gospel of Mark, and you see the arrest of Jesus, there is someone described who is nameless that runs to safety. A lot of Bible scholars believe that this nameless figure is Mark himself.

Mark would have been close to Jesus and would have learned a lot from him. But Mark never seems to want to make a name for himself. The gospel account that is attributed to him doesn't even bear his name. Mark was pleased just for people to know Jesus and did not care much for people to know him.

This is the perfect disposition of a follower of Jesus. We need to be men who do not seek to leave a legacy for ourselves. It is not important that we build up a kingdom with our name. Our brand, our logo, or our prominence have no real value in the grand scheme of things. The one thing that matters the most is that the world knows Jesus. Our highest goal in life is to make great the name of our savior.

Oh, how our lives would be different if we adopted the mentality of Mark. And this is really Jesus' mentality. At least, that is how Paul describes it in Philippians. He says that the mind of Jesus is one of humility, humility even to the point of death on the cross. It lets us take up the same posture as Mark, who simply emulates the posture of his Lord.

Take time to examine your life and what your goals are. In what ways are they helping you to accomplish this mission? And in what ways are they promoting the name of Jesus more than they are promoting your own name? As you look at your life, prayerfully consider what needs to change. The Holy Spirit will surely be there along the way to reveal those things to you. And by the grace of God, you can make the changes necessary to live a life similar to Mark. One that does not seek your own glory but seeks the glory of a greater one.

REFLECTION

Day 1: What admirable qualities are there in Mark's life?

Day 2: Why is popularity so important to us?

Day 3: Is it important for us to leave a Legacy?

Day 4: What kind of legacy should we strive to leave?

Day 5: If you were to die today with legacy, would you leave?

Day 6: What do you need to change your life in order to improve your legacy?

Day 7: Write a letter to someone that you hope is impacted by your life.

PRAYER REQUESTS

ANSWERED PRAYERS

Week 46
Andrew - Come and See

""Come," he replied, "and you will see." So they went and saw where he was staying, and they spent that day with him. It was about four in the afternoon."
John 1:39

Read John 1

There are evangelism strategies in this world. You can go to a Christian bookstore, and there will be shelves full of books that tell you how to share your Faith. However, I think that the best evangelism strategy out there can be found simply by looking at Andrew's life. Andrew was my brother. The reason that Peter ever came to know Jesus was because of Andrew's evangelistic effort.

Was Andrew's secret? You may think that he had an elaborate 12-point plan that helped him to clearly articulate the gospel or to defend his faith in difficult circumstances. But that is simply not the case. And Evangelism was as simple as it gets. I like to call it come and see evangelism. An encounter with Jesus. And by the end of his time with him, he was convinced that Jesus was the son of God. He was amazed by his teaching and what he was able to do. And so, Andrew ran to his brother Peter. And he told Peter to simply come and see. That was it. Come and see for yourself. This makes me think of the Bible verse that says come taste and see that the Lord is good. That is what Andrew invited his brother to do that day. And that is exactly what he did. He came, he saw, and he experienced the life-changing love of Jesus.

Have we overcomplicated what it means to share the gospel? I would say that we have. We skip over the simplest and most effective step because we are so worried about trying to find our presentation. Now, to be fair, we do not have a physical Jesus to whom we can bring our friends.

So, what do we do in light of this passage scripture? Although we do not have a physical Jesus, we do have Jesus in the scriptures. We can bring people to Jesus by showing them him in the word. This may mean that you are there for them when they have questions about the Bible, then you show them to him. This may simply mean you hand them a gospel tract that has the word of God on it. This may mean that you invite your friends and your coworkers to come to church with you so they can hear from the ward of God alongside you. That is one of the best forms of evangelism. Invite someone to come with you and then take them out to lunch afterward so you can discuss what was talked about.

When you do this, a few things will happen that don't normally happen. Is that your friend will go somewhere brand new and intimidating with someone that they know and trust. The second is that your friend will have someone to help interpret what is going on for them. And finally, your friend will have someone who can personally share the gospel with them when it can be very intimidating to try to learn some of that importance from an unknown source. Do not neglect the simple act of coming and see if Angel follows in the footsteps of our brother and fellow saint Andrew.

REFLECTION

Day 1: Have you ever learned an evangelistic strategy?

Day 2: Why do people not share the gospel as often as they ought to?

Day 3: Have you ever shared with someone?

Day 4: What makes Come and See Evangelism so effective?

Day 5: What are the shortcomings of this type of evangelistic strategy?

Day 6: Who in your life do you need to invite to come see Jesus?

Day 7: How do you plan to invite them?

he gave what is called the Great Commission. It is one of the great missions of the church. Jesus tells his disciples to go and make other disciples by baptizing them and teaching them all that Jesus taught them. This is the essence of disciple-making. It is to help other people follow Jesus more closely.

Paul did it with Timothy and others. But this is not just the work reserved for a missionary, a pastor, or an evangelist. This is basic Christianity. This is what it means to be a disciple.

That naturally leads us to the next question. Are you being a disciple who makes other disciples? Are you helping other people to follow Jesus more closely? If you are not, then I'm going to encourage you to repent of your sins. This is the fundamental task of the Christian. To fail to attempt disciple-making is to fall into sin.

I am not saying that if you are not good at making disciples, then you are. I am saying that if you don't try to make disciples, then you are sending. And you may be asking yourself how? How does someone make a disciple of someone else? The answer is similar to the task. Anything that you can do to help someone else follow Jesus is a disciple-making. For some of the readers of this book, it will be leading someone through a Bible study. For other readers, it may simply be an encouragement to someone else. For even more still, it may be being a hospital person in your community and inviting people into your home and into your life. All of these are different ways that you can go about making disciples. The one thing that you cannot do is neglect the task altogether. So, how will you follow in the footsteps of Paul and Timothy? How will you make disciples?

REFLECTION

Day 1: What is a disciple?

Day 2: Have you ever been disciplined by somebody?

Day 3: Have you ever made a disciple?

Day 4: What keeps you from making disciples?

Day 5: Who is your natural sphere of influence that you could begin to pour into?

Day 6: What kind of lessons could you teach them about Jesus?

Day 7: What kind of resources do you need to gather for this?

PRAYER REQUESTS

ANSWERED PRAYERS

WEEK 49
JOHN - THE BELOVED

"Come near to God and he will come near to you. Wash your hands, you sinners, and purify your hearts, you double-minded."
JAMES 4:8

Read John 21

Who is your best friend? We all have one. The person that we are closer to than anyone else. If you are married, then I hope your answer is your spouse. Your best friend is the person who knows you the best and who you trust the most. This does not mean that you don't have other friends. And it does not mean that you don't have other close friends. But by definition, you can only have one best friend. You can only have one person that is closer than the rest.

Jesus seemed to have a best friend. Did you know that? Jesus had 12 followers that he called his disciples. We have learned a lot about them so far. But within the 12 disciples, he had seemed to be an inner circle. Over and over again, Jesus pulls Peter, James, and John off to the side to have special and more intimate conversations than he does with the others. However, even among those three, there seems to be a unique and special relationship between Jesus and John.

John is called the disciple whom Jesus loved. None of the other disciples get that kind of scripture in the scriptures. John is the one who sits next to Jesus at the Last Supper. He is the one who rests his head on Jesus 's shoulder during the meal. To describe the relationship in a simple way, simply call them best friends.

At first, when I think about this, I envy John. I envy his closeness to Jesus and his opportunity to learn from him in a more intimate way than it seems like anyone else gets to. I am tempted to ask myself. What makes John so special?

And then I am reminded of the wonderful truth that we know from the Bible. That all of us have an intimately close relationship with Jesus now that he has ascended to heaven. Because he promised that when he ascended into heaven, he would send down his Holy Spirit to live with us. We have Jesus as close as he can possibly get to us.

But I am still troubled by the question of whether, if we were sitting around the table at a heavenly banquet, there would be a seat next to him for me. Would there be a seat next to him for you? You see, I am wondering if I am taking advantage of the potential intimacy that I could have with my savior. When I think about it critically, I realize that the closeness that could be there is not there because I have not seen it out. And so, I am asking you as you read this week. Have you sought out a deeper and closer relationship with Jesus? If you haven't, Friend, it is available to you. U2 is a beloved disciple.

REFLECTION

Day 1: How did John become so intimate with Jesus?

Day 2: What do you think their conversations were like?

Day 3: How close are you to Jesus?

Day 4: What can you do to get closer to him?

Day 5: Why is it important that Jesus had a best friend?

Day 6: Who is your best friend?

Day 7: Does that person know Jesus as you do?

PRAYER REQUESTS

ANSWERED PRAYERS

Week 50
Thomas - Doubter

"So do not fear, for I am with you; do not be dismayed,
for I am your God. I will strengthen you and help you;
I will uphold you with my righteous right hand."
Isaiah 41:10

Read John 20

I have often been encouraged by the late pastor, Timothy Keller. He was an incredible thinker and theologian. He was a great pastor and leader for his church family. And in the way that he helped me the most, he was a great writer. One of the books that he wrote was called The Reason for God. It was a book aimed at doubters and skeptics of the Christian faith. Keller was able to write such a book because, at one point was a doubter and a skeptic. His spiritual journey is an incredible one to read about and see how the Lord formed him over the years.

I appreciate Keller's honesty in his life and in the book The Reason for God because I have had doubts, too. I have had my questions about the Christian faith. I am sure that you have felt the same kind of skepticism from time to time. I have wondered where the miracles are recorded in scripture, which is actually true. Jesus says life is as incredible as the Bible claims it is. Did he actually rise from the grave? What if I'm wrong?

When I am faced with these doubts and these questions, I remember Thomas's story. Thomas was someone who struggled with doubt. Even with the resurrected Jesus standing right in front of him, Thomas still had doubts about whether or not Jesus was who he said he was. He was more ready to believe that Jesus might be a ghost than resurrected. That was until Jesus told Thomas to take his hand and put it on his side to see the wounds that were left there and to feel the scars that were made by the Roman soldiers.

Once Thomas had the opportunity to see and touch and feel and know that he was indeed the resurrected Christ, then he finally claimed to believe. But even in his claim of belief, he makes a plea to ask God to help him in his unbelief. What an incredible thing to see in the word of God. Even after seeing, hearing, and touching the resurrected son of God, they're still lingering in unbelief.

Friend, if you are like me and have struggled with doubt, then you are in good company. One of Jesus' own disciples struggled openly with doubt. And he was not turned away. He was not scorned for his unbelief. He was welcomed in to see what was true. And so, when you are struggling with your doubt and unbelief, do not run from Jesus seeking other answers. Run to him. Let him show you the truth. Let him remind you of why you began to believe in the first place.

Tim Keller's book is not the only one out there that can help you with your struggling Faith. There are many great apologists that you can read and hear different arguments about why you can confidently believe in the Bible, in the life and death of Jesus, and in his glorious resurrection. It would benefit you, Friend, to take Tom to research and read books like these.

REFLECTION

Day 1: Have you ever had doubts about the Christian faith?

Day 2: Why were those doubts there?

Day 3: What happened to help those doubts go away?

Day 4: Do you know someone who is having doubts right now?

Day 5: How can you help remove those doubts?

Day 6: Are there any books or resources that have helped you when you doubted?

Day 7: What is the significance of Thomas's saying I believe Help my unbelief?

PRAYER REQUESTS

ANSWERED PRAYERS

WEEK 51

JUDAS - BETRAYER

"For God so loved the world that he gave his one and only Son, that whoever believes in him shall not perish but have eternal life."
JOHN 3:16

Read Matthew 26

There are certain names that seem to have been removed from history because of an individual. For example, there are not many people named Adolf any longer. I don't know of anyone who would bear the last name Hitler anymore. There are not many women who are naming their daughters Jezebel. Because of the scandal that surrounds these names and the people who bore them in history, we shy away from them.

One name is the name of Judas. What was a very common name in biblical times has now become very uncommon. Even among the 12 disciples, there were two of them named Judas. This is why the gospel writers had to clarify each time whether they were talking about Judas Iscariot or not. You see, Judas did something so heinous and so condemnable that people fear to even bear his name any longer. Judas betrayed Jesus. For a small amount of money, Judas sold Jesus out. He led the Roman guards right to him in the garden of death. He betrayed him with a kiss. And he watched and counted his money as the Roman guards arrested, beat, mocked, and crucified his master.

When you read the gospel account that shows, in detail, the betrayal that Judas plays on Jesus, you probably had a similar reaction to me. When I read that account, I was filled with rage and anger. I am baffled that someone so close to Jesus could be so far from him spiritually.

It doesn't seem possible that someone who sat under his teaching every day for three years and saw the miracles that he performed was able to deny him. And not just to deny him but to sell him out. To betray him. Surely, the devil was in the works because this simply does not make sense.

If you were filled with anger, I want to warn you, Friend. That not much separates you from Judas. Not much separates me from Judas. In fact, the only thing that separates us from anyone who now has a name that no one else would share is the Grace of God. The only thing different between you and me and anyone else who does not follow. Jesus is God's intervention in their lives. It is all because of God's amazing grace that we know him, love him, and trust him. Had he not come after us, we surely would not have gone after him.

And the more incredible truth for us to consider this week is not just how bad Judas was, but also what we have been saved from. It is that God would save even Judas. Had Judas placed his faith in Jesus, his only God's son, and truly loved him with his whole heart, God would have saved him. Even after the betrayal and the counting of money, God would have saved him. Because God desires all men to come to know him. God does not want anyone to perish in their sin. Every single person is only one step away from eternal life. And the next time you attempt to judge someone for their sin, be reminded that there is no such thing as being too far gone for our God.

REFLECTION

Day 1: Why does no one name their children Judas?

Day 2: Have you ever been betrayed?

Day 3: Were you able to forgive that person? Why or why not?

Day 4: What would need to happen in order for you to forgive them?

Day 5: Why would Jesus forgive Judas?

Day 6: What does that teach us about God?

Day 7: Is there anyone in your life that you are unwilling to forgive?

PRAYER REQUESTS

ANSWERED PRAYERS

WEEK 52

BARNABAS - ENCOURAGER

"Therefore encourage one another and build each other up, just as in fact you are doing."
1 THESSALONIANS 5:11

Read Acts 4

Well, friends, we have nearly spent a whole year together. If you have kept on track, then you are on week 52 of a year-long study of God 's word. You have powered through and met some of the most amazing men of God through the Bible. You have learned all kinds of lessons about what it means to follow Jesus and how to be more like him. I hope that you have been encouraged by the word. That is something that I say a lot at my own church gatherings. Because this is what it is all about for us as believers. We are made to encourage one another in the word of God.

This is why I wanted our final session together to be considering the person of Barnabas. Barnabas has his name because he was an encourager. He was someone who would stick by the underdog and champion him until he finally figured things out. Barnabas and Paul had their issues along the way because they had a dispute over the person of John Mark. You see, John Mark had left Paul in the middle of a missionary journey. We don't know why he left. He could've gotten homesick. He could've gotten actually sick. He could've just simply given up and thrown in the towel. When they all reconvene together, Paul said that he would not take another trip with John Mark. Barnabas understood the reasoning but still wasn't encourager. Barnabas said that he would take John Mark under his wing and take him on his next missionary journey. The fact that that moment had an impact on Mark's life is hard to calculate. But we can see the end result.

By the end of Paul's life, he writes that he would command John Mark on any mission trip. He calls him to be a good and faithful brother. This is largely because of the work that Barnabas put in. Barnabas encouraged John Mark when no one else would. At his lowest moment, when he was probably ready to give up on serving the Lord as a missionary, Barnabas stepped in. He encouraged him with the Lord of God. Perhaps Barnabas told him that the Lord would never leave him nor forsake him. Maybe he reminded him of the promise at the end of the great commission that Jesus will be with us always, even to the end of the age. Whatever he did and whatever he said, it accomplished an amazing thing. Someone was encouraged by the word.

There is definitely someone in your life who needs to be encouraged by the word. Would you be the person that brings that encouraging word to them? Would you be the one who sends them the text that they need to read? Would you be the one who writes them a note and put it in the mail today? Would you be the one who shares with them and encourages social media posts? Be like Barnabas. Rather, it would be like the one who Barnabas was in bodying. Be like Jesus, the greatest encourager of them all. The one who would reach down into the depths of society. The one who lifts the low heads of the discouraged. Be an encourager in the word.

REFLECTION

Day 1: Why is encouragement important in life?

Day 2: Do you have someone in your life that is an encouragement to you?

Day 3: Is there someone who you should be encouraging more?

Day 4: What would change in your life if you spent more time encouraging people?

Day 5: What lessons do you learn about Christianity when you read about Barnabas?

Day 6: Have you ever stood up for the underdog?

Day 7: What happened when you invested in someone like that?

PRAYER REQUESTS

ANSWERED PRAYERS

Printed in Great Britain
by Amazon

53310309R00126